Astrology and Interior Design
Unlocking the Secret to Your Personal Style at Home

Copyright © 2014 by Kita Marie Williams

ISBN: 978-0-615-99970-8

All rights reserved. No part of this publication may be reproduced, distributed, or transmitted in any form or by any means, including photocopying, recording, or other electronic or mechanical methods, without the prior written permission of the publisher, except in the case of brief quotations embodied in critical reviews and certain other noncommercial uses permitted by copyright law. For permission requests, write to the publisher, addressed "Attention: Kita Marie Williams," at the address below.

Kita Marie Williams
468 N Camden Dr., Suite 222
Beverly Hills, CA 90210
www.kitamariewilliams.com

Third Edition

This book is dedicated to all of my readers and their open hearts and minds. It is through study, observation and curiosity that real breakthroughs are made. Keep your hearts open to the new and mysterious and your minds poised to master the unknown.

Table of Contents

Preface

Introduction:

- Astrology Basics
- What You Need to Know Before You Get Started
- How to Use This Book

1. The Aries Home
2. The Taurus Home
3. The Gemini Home
4. The Cancer Home
5. The Leo Home
6. The Virgo Home
7. The Libra Home
8. The Scorpio Home
9. The Sagittarius Home
10. The Capricorn Home
11. The Aquarius Home
12. The Pisces Home
13. What You've Learned and How to Use It
    - Your Personal Design and Décor Guide

References

Photo Credits

Preface

In March of 2012, I answered a phone call that changed my life. A very successful man had a temporary living situation in a luxury apartment and had absolutely no idea how to furnish or decorate it. A really close friend of mine gave him my name and number as a professional decorator (Thank you BETTY!). At the time, I had been unemployed and struggling to make ends meet and being a full-time interior designer was simply a dream.

Nevertheless, with that single phone call, the universe had hit the fast forward button and my dream suddenly became a reality overnight. That month I started my interior design, decoration and home staging company, KMW Interiors, and I have been happily working in the career of my dreams ever since.

So, how does Astrology factor in? I can tell you that the stars have been a major theme in my life from the very beginning. The earliest memory I can recall as a baby is of the stars in the night sky. I honestly cannot remember anything before that. And as it turns out, the stars have been something I've gravitated toward all of my natural life.

Over the course of my career, I took advantage of my knack for knowing people's style and preferences by examining their birth chart. In fact, I started using birth charts to help me plan out a design and decoration scheme for my clients from the start. It was a natural thing for me and helped me not only create beautiful spaces that were unique to each client, but also helped my clients discover more about themselves.

I wanted to write this book because many of my clients and friends are very interested in my techniques and would like to discover on their own how to decorate or organize their space. I figured if my clients, friends and family think that combining Astrology and interior design is fun, interesting and useful, maybe other people around the world will as well. And now, here it is! My first book!

Astrology & Interior Design: *Unlocking the Secret to your Personal Style at Home* is designed to show supposed styles and design elements that would be preferred by each Zodiac sign and provide the information in a way that the reader can reference easily. You can skip around the book or read it all. You can reference signs of a specific element or read the signs of a specific quality like house rulership or whether it's cardinal, fixed or mutable. It really is up to you. The most important thing is that you have fun with it and hopefully discover more about your tastes and preferences.

Lastly, even though I've been studying astrology and interior design for over 15 years, I still consider myself a student that will never graduate. I want to keep learning forever and share my knowledge and observations with you. I plan on creating more than one edition of this book so that I can update it with new styles, trends and astrological discoveries. I also plan on writing more books about interior design in general.

Thank you for purchasing this book and I hope you enjoy it!

Introduction

Decorators and interior designers are taught certain basics about how design can affect a person on a psychological level. Subjects like color psychology and the art of object placement help professionals understand, in broad terms, how to create a particular type of energy in a space and these techniques can be quite effective. However, these subjects do not explain why a particular person might have a positive reaction to the color red while another person may have a negation reaction. When it comes to an interior space, why is it that color, lighting and overall style can affect different people in different ways? What is the root of someone's innate reaction to their environment? Obviously, each person is different and their life experiences, personality traits and the influence of trends can all shape an individual's taste. The root of understanding a persons' style lies in getting to know them on a deeper level.

For many, astrology provides an interesting and entertaining conduit for understanding some aspects of how and why a person may have certain personality traits and preferences. Many enjoy using the insights of astrology for personal discovery and to perhaps understand friends and loved ones. Although it is not considered a science, astrology has an ancient history and mystery that many really enjoy. You would be hard pressed to find a person that has not heard of or is not familiar with astrology on some level. Just ask a stranger on the street what their sign is and they are likely to respond with an answer.

Since a physical space can affect someone personally, the insights from astrology can most certainly be applied to create a set of guidelines that may help a homeowner, designer or decorator create a space that enhances an individual's wellbeing. Knowing how colors, textures and even an established decorative style might affect an individual can serve to help bring success to décor and design projects.

This is meant to be a fun and informative book that will highlight each of the Zodiac signs and offer suggestions on how a home can be designed, organized and decorated to please the tastes and preferences of an individual that has major influences of that particular sign. The first twelve chapters are dedicated to one sign, so that you can easily navigate to the chapter where the sign of interest is discussed. Each chapter offers design and decoration suggestions for the main areas of the home. These areas include: the living room, the kitchen and dining space, the bedroom and the bathroom.

Astrology Basics

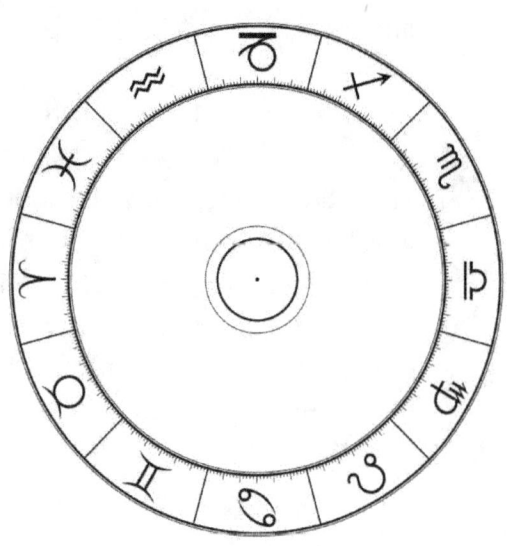

Astrology is an ancient and complex study that encompasses many nuances and schools of practice. Obviously, this book cannot cover all of that information, so brief descriptions and general information is provided. However, by the end of this portion of the book, you should have a strong enough foundation to explore more on your own. If you already have basic knowledge of astrology you can skip ahead and dive right into the chapters on your Sun sign, Ascendant sign and Fourth House sign(s).

1. What is astrology?
   - "**Astrology** consists of several systems of divination based on the premise that there is a relationship between astronomical phenomena and events in the human world."[1]
   - There are various systems of astrology, but for our purposes we will be using **traditional western astrology**".[2]

2. The Zodiac
   - "In both astrology and historical astronomy, the zodiac (Greek: ζῳδιακός, zōidiakos) is a circle of twelve 30° divisions of celestial longitude that are centered upon the ecliptic: the apparent path of the Sun across the celestial sphere over the course of the year."[3]

   - Each of the twelve 30° divisions represents a sign and each sign is derived from celestial star formations called constellations.

---

[1] Definition provided by Wikipedia: http://en.wikipedia.org/wiki/Astrology
[2] For more information on the different systems of astrology, reading Wikipedia's full description: http://en.wikipedia.org/wiki/Astrology
[3] This definition is referenced from Wikipedia: http://en.wikipedia.org/wiki/Zodiac

3. *The Twelve Signs*
    - The table below lists each of the Zodiac signs, their symbols/symbolic figures and the longitudinal position of each sign's cusp (or starting point). This chart does not go into the characteristics of the Sun sign. That will be included in the beginning of each chapter that discusses that particular sign.

Chart of the Twelve Signs

Sun Sign Name	Symbol	Longitude	Birth Date Ranges
Aries	♈ The Ram	0°	21 March – 20 April
Taurus	♉ The Bull	30°	21 April – May 21
Gemini	♊ The Twins	60°	22 May – 21 June
Cancer	♋ The Crab	90°	22 June – 22 July
Leo	♌ The Lion	120°	23 July – 22 August
Virgo	♍ The Virgin	150°	23 August – 23 September
Libra	♎ The Scales	180°	24 September – 23 October
Scorpio	♏ The Scorpion	210°	24 October – 22 November
Sagittarius	♐ The Archer	240°	23 November – 21 December
Capricorn	♑ The Goat	270°	22 December – 20 January
Aquarius	♒ The Water-Bearer	300°	21 January – 19 February
Pisces	♓ The Fishes	330°	20 February – 20 March[4]

---

[4] The information in this chart was referenced from Wikipedia: http://en.wikipedia.org/wiki/Zodiac#The_twelve_signs

The Elements

Each sign in the Zodiac is associated with an element that describes the vital energy of the sign. These elements include: Fire, Water, Air and Earth. The energy of these elements is part of the personality and life circumstances of the sign that possesses it. Consequently, it is an important part of a person's taste and design preference. Below is a brief description of each element. After each section, there is a footnote that shows you where you can go online to get more information on each of these elements. For our purposes, these short descriptions will do.

Fire

The signs Aries, Leo and Sagittarius are Fire signs.

Fire signs are bold, courageous and a bit larger than life. Like the element fire itself, fire sign people can be quite wild and hard to tame. They tend to be very ego driven and forceful when it comes to having their way. Fiery people are typically very passionate and can be vary ardent lovers or friends. There passionate and commanding style can easily be represented in their preferences in style and décor. Passionate and bold colors are often chosen in the home and well as items that seem to show movement and dynamism.[5]

Water

The signs Cancer, Scorpio and Pisces are Water signs.

Like water, these people seem to flow through life and are driven by their emotions. They are rather sensitive, perceptive and very intuitive. Watery people's feelings run deep and they are usually unafraid to express their emotions as, most of the time, they simply cannot avoid doing so. For the typical water sign person, home is a very private place where their delicate feelings can be protected and nurtured. Gentle fabrics and soothing colors are generally preferred by those who are a water sign.[6]

---

[5] For more information on the Fire signs, visit: http://www.astrology.com/fire-0/2-d-d-67460
[6] For more information on the Water signs, visit: http://www.astrology.com/water/2-d-d-67461

Air

The signs Gemini, Libra and Aquarius are Air signs.

Those born under this this element are usually very good at communication and tend to be very intellectual in their approach to life. They love to learn and feel quite restless if they aren't given new information to absorb. At home, the Air sign person is chatty and prefers company to solitude, so you'll notice the environment is people-friendly and accommodating to guests. Air signs also love open spaces, so larger windows that can be opened to let in fresh air are essential.[7]

Earth

The signs Taurus, Virgo and Capricorn are Earth signs

Earth sign individuals are very practical, responsible, realistic and reliable. These people love the physical comforts in life and usually don't take any risks. In fact, they are likely to go for a goal that is attainable by calculated and time-tested methods. Their homes are likely to be very comfortable and practical leaning more toward traditional style and décor. Earth tones and wood elements would likely be present in the home.[8]

---

[7] For more information on the Air signs, visit: http://www.astrology.com/air/2-d-d-67446
[8] For more information on the Earth signs, visit: http://www.astrology.com/earth/2-d-d-67459

What You Need To Know Before You Get Started

Your Sun Sign

Your sun sign essentially represents the sign on the zodiac the sun was positioned in on the day of your birth. To find your sun sign simply look at the "Chart of the Twelve Signs" in the "Astrology Basics" section of this book (page 10), scan the "Birth Date Ranges" column and see what range your birth date falls in on the chart. For example, if your birthday is July 19th, then you fall in the date range for Cancer. This means that on the day of your birth, the Sun was located in the sign of Cancer, hence, this is your Sun sign.

Your Ascendant (Rising) Sign

Merriam Webster's Dictionary describes the ascendant as "the point of the ecliptic or degree of the zodiac that rises above the eastern horizon at any moment"[9]. This is basically the point in the sky where the eastern horizon line was located or was "rising" on the day you were born. This reference point or line is determined by the location you are on planet earth and the time of day you were born. Both the location and the time of your birth can be found on your birth certificate. Or, you simply can ask your mother. Most mothers find the location, date and birth time easy to remember. After all, it was a major event for both of you!

Obviously, the ascendant is a bit more complicated to calculate. So, included is a list of two great places online to get a free birth chart. These sites have applications that can calculate where the horizon line was when you were born and render an entire birth chart for you. A personal birth chart is a useful tool to have if you plan to investigate more about astrology and your personal stars.

Free Birth Chart Resources

Website Name	Description	Link
Café Astrology	*Provides free birth charts and information on various transits and personal birth chart aspects*	www.cafeastro.com
Astro.com	*Very useful site for making various types of charts. Subscriptions are also available*	www.astro.com

---

[9] Description taken from Merriam-Webster's online dictionary: http://www.merriam-webster.com/dictionary/ascendent

Your Fourth House Cusp

When you finally have your chart, you will notice that it is divided into twelve sections. Each of these sections represents a "house" and each house rules a particular aspect of your personal life. For our purposes, you will need to find where your fourth house begins or the "cusp" of your fourth house. The fourth house rules your home and family life, so it will be helpful to know what Zodiac sign(s) are influencing this portion of your chart. Does your fourth house include more than one sign? If so, be sure to read not only your Sun and Ascendant sign chapters, but also the chapters on the sign(s) that are in your fourth house.

Sun Sign vs. Ascendant/Rising Sign

In traditional astrology, the sun is the most important celestial body in a person's birth chart. The sign the sun is located in at the time of your birth represents your inner yearnings or desires you have on a very personal level that are only known by close friends and family. Most horoscopes focus on the Sun sign when predicting moods and trends. However, this is not very accurate for most people. It also begs the question; how could all of the people of a particular sun sign experience the same thing? More often than not, they do not. This is where the ascendant can offer a clearer picture.

The ascendant sign represents the outer circumstances or the "earthly" situation you may find yourself experiencing. This is the outer "you" or the "face" you show the world while the sun sign is the side of you that's internal and is not always representative of what people perceive about you in reality. For example, one can be a Capricorn by sun sign and display many of the characteristics of a Capricorn. They are very hard-working, responsible, understand limitations and in some ways, are very traditional. In contrast, a Capricorn with an Aquarius ascendant sign will have outer influences that may lead them toward more humanitarian and non-traditional situations, beliefs and people. If this person were purely a Capricorn by nature, they would likely miss out on experiences and knowledge due to an adherence to tradition. However, due to the general influence of the ascendant sign, outer circumstances will expose this individual to interesting situations and people that take them out of their Capricorn shell.

Consequently, ascendant sign experiences will certainly influence your preferences in many ways. What one may seek on an inner level, as represented by the sun sign, is colored by the rich experiences they have as a person from their rising sign. In conclusion, the combination of your sun sign and ascendant sign helps to create your unique life experiences and preferences.

How to Use This Book

The proceeding twelve chapters will represent each of the twelve signs of the Zodiac. Each chapter will outline general characteristics of each sign and follow-up with basic representative design and décor elements for that particular sign. At this point you should know your sun sign, your ascendant sign and the signs that affect your fourth house, which will help determine the chapters that are the most relevant for you. Read the design elements of the sun sign first. Take note of the things that you like. Of course, there will be some suggestions for your sign that you do not agree with. At which point, you should take a look at the chapters that discuss your ascendant/rising sign and the sign(s) in your fourth house.

At the end of this book, there is a sample worksheet titled "Your Personal Design & Décor Guide" provided that is modeled as a guide to help you organize all of the preferred design elements from reading your sun sign, ascendant sign and fourth house sign(s). If you have the eBook version of this book, you can use the worksheet at the end as a model for creating your own worksheet by hand on a sheet of paper or as template to create your own word table file. If you have purchased the paperback print version of this book, you can simply take notes on the worksheet provided at the end. It is recommended that you make copies of the worksheet so that you can use it more than once for other people. Once you fill this out, you will have a great foundation of colors, decor and styles that can be used on your own, or provided to a professional as a reference. Treat this book as a great starting point for creating a home that is truly reflective of your taste and that gives you a feeling of comfort.

Further Personal Investigation

This book is designed to give the reader a glimpse into how the celestial characteristics of their unique birth chart play out in their preferences for their personal space. Someone new to Astrology may have many questions. For example, someone might wonder, why am I attracted to fire sign style when I'm a water sign? Why do I like the style of a Cancer (ruled by the Moon) when I'm a Sagittarius and (ruled by Jupiter)? That's where the birth chart you created can help you in your investigation.

If this book sparks curiosity and the desire to learn more about your personal chart, there are many resources online and in books that can help you on your quest. It can be very intriguing to watch the true you unfold as you research your personal birth chart. If you are new to Astrology, I hope this book not only helps you to find a great starting point for creating a space that nurtures your soul, but also sparks a desire to learn more about your life journey and how you can live it in a way that is more fulfilling.

Chapter 1: **The Aries Home**

ARIES

Aries Description
Element: Fire
Sign Quality: Cardinal
Ruling Planet: Mars
Zodiac House: First House of the Self
Corporeal Representation: The Head, Brain, Eyes & Face

Aries is the first sign of the zodiac, and true to being first, it is a pioneering sign that loves action, energy and trying new things. Represented by the Ram and action planet Mars, an Aries person is often bold, brave and enthusiastic. The Aries native thinks of the "self" first and is quite aware of this. Yet, that doesn't mean that they are selfish. They are simply more aware of the fact that they cannot help anyone else if their personal needs are not met first.

Starting projects is a common activity for an Aries. They love to create new ideas or be the first to try a new thing. However, the pull of the next big thing is often too hard for the Aries to resist and they are quick to leave a project and move on. Venture capitalism and entrepreneurial endeavors are the prefect careers for the true Aries.

The Fire Element and the Aries Home

Because Aries is a Fire sign, the native Aries usually responds quite positively to bold fiery colors in the home. Colors like red and red-orange are fitting for areas where the Aries would gather with friends and family. These colors are naturally energetic and help the active Aries find inspiration. The color should be used strategically; however, as too much bold red in a space can be overwhelming, even for an active Aries.

Metal objects are perfect for the Aries home as well. Metal is a material that can be transformed by fire, so it is fitting that such a material would have a place the home of a fiery Aries. Try to incorporate items that give the impression of movement when choosing metal decorations or furniture.

Since Aries is a Mars-ruled action sign, dynamics should be incorporated where possible. Furniture and knick-knacks with moving parts help sustain the energy of movement and change that drives an Aries. However, there are some spaces where too much movement should be avoided, such as the bedroom and the bathroom.

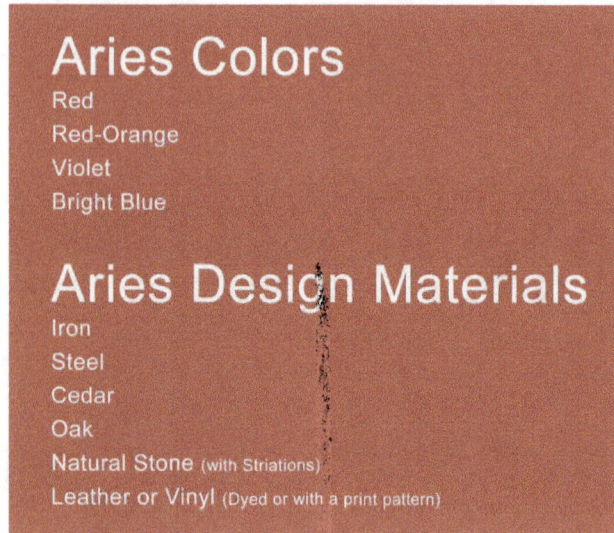

Aries Colors
Red
Red-Orange
Violet
Bright Blue

Aries Design Materials
Iron
Steel
Cedar
Oak
Natural Stone (with Striations)
Leather or Vinyl (Dyed or with a print pattern)

The Aries Living Room

The living space for an Aries is a place where they can socialize and find inspiration. The furniture should be comfortable, but interesting. Mid-century modern style usually suits the native Aries. It is simple and modern, yet has interesting shapes. Pieces designed by the architect and furniture designer Mies Van Der Rohe (who, in fact, was an Aries) would be great in an Aries home since many of Van Der Rohe's pieces feature curved metal parts that simulate movement.

Furniture pieces do not have to be large. The busy Aries typically moves around in the home and would do a lot of chatting standing up. Furniture should be moderate in size to give the Aries room to move around freely. Major furniture pieces, such as the sofa or sectional should be basic in color. Black, white or a neutral color would be best.

In this living space, pops of bold red and violet add energy and interest. The larger furniture pieces are white and simple. The sofa and the tables use metal for the legs.

However, the accents like throws and pillows should be a bold color, ideally, a shade of red. Strategic pops of red, violet or bright blue on an accent wall, simple chair or ottoman would be enough to infuse interest and energy in the room.

The Aries Kitchen and Dining Space

Most people that are of the sign of Aries are too busy exploring new restaurants and hot spots to spend time in the Kitchen, so the kitchen doesn't need to be very large. A small kitchen with all of the necessary basic equipment would suit an Aries just fine. However, the general design of the kitchen should be clean, uncluttered and feel exciting enough to inspire an Aries to actually spend time in it.

Note the basic pallet of black and white with bold red as an accent. The offset placement of the upper red cabinets creates a feeling of movement. The detailing of the backsplash adds energy as well.

A dynamic design incorporated in the backsplash would work well in the kitchen, especially one that runs horizontally across the wall. Red accents like pots, and counter top appliances would add some style and provide basic functions. An Aries would also appreciate the attractiveness of stainless steel appliances in the space.

Independence is important to an Aries, so an Aries host would feel more comfortable if quests helped themselves to whatever they needed. Both the kitchen and the dining area should make it easy for people to grab what they need themselves. A nice portable bar fully stocked with anything a guest would need to make a drink would be perfect.

The Aries would likely not use a separate dining area as much; so, an open concept kitchen dining space would work perfectly. Since most open concept kitchen dining areas tend to be small, a glass dining table would be ideal. The glass top would make more of the small space visible and give the illusion of spaciousness. Dining chairs don't have to be as comfortable, so you can pick designs that add panache and concentrate less on comfort.

The Aries Bedroom

The go-getter Aries needs to rest, but they still function better when there is excitement in the bedroom as well. The general atmosphere of the bedroom should be bright and have plenty of sunlight when needed. Spaciousness is also important so that the native Aries can roam around. The room needs to feel uncluttered and offer free movement around the bed.

Red is used here, but is in small accents. The wall art and decal provide great focal points and complement the color scheme.

Red can be used in very small accent pieces, but should not be too prominent. A shade of blue or violet would work better for the bedroom since these colors are a lower energy than red. When choosing bedding, try to go for simple and modern styles. Solid colors would work best. If you must use prints, pick a simple yet sophisticated pattern and pair it with coordinating solid colors to temper the energy of the print.

If you can avoid having a lot of furniture pieces in the bedroom, that would be best. A large bed and two nightstands would be simple and work well. Most of an Aries' clothes should be located in a centralized area such as a wardrobe or closet. If you could avoid having a dresser, that would be ideal. Aries rules the head, so a system to store and/or display the collection of head gear would be a great extra.

The Aries Bathroom

Like the kitchen, the bathroom is a place where an Aries would not spend a huge amount of time. An Aries does, however, want a bathroom that is clean and serene. A neutral toned bathroom with blue or jade green accents would make a great color scheme. You could model an Aries bathroom after one you would find in a health club including a system of stocked towels with a receptacle below where used towels can be thrown. Toiletries should be centrally located and easily accessed since the Aries wants showers to be quick and efficient.

For the male Aries, a spacious shower without a tub would do just fine. Most women, regardless of their sign appreciate a soaking tub. Although an Aries woman may not spend as much time in the tub. It would mostly be used as therapy for sore muscles brought on by sports or vigorous daily activities and not as much for a lazy relaxation session.

This bathroom is spacious with a bright and energetic accent color. The feel is simple and serene with a few details to add interest.

Chapter 2: The Taurus Home

TAURUS

Taurus Description
Element: Earth
Sign Quality: Fixed
Ruling Planet: Venus
Zodiac House: Second House of Income & Values
Corporeal Representation: The Neck, Throat, Jawbone Larnyx, Chin, Ears & Tongue

Taurus is the second sign of the Zodiac and those of this sun sign are known to be steadfast, resolute and a bit stubborn. As an Earth sign, Taurus is very practical and sensible, yet loves to be surrounded by beauty. Ruled by the planet Venus, the native Taurus is a very sensual sign that craves creature comforts. Good food, fine clothes and priceless works of art are serious temptations for the true Taurus.

When it comes to work, you can count on a Taurus. They are very responsible and are results driven. When a Taurus does a job, they expect a reward, so if you have a Taurus working for you, be sure to give them responsibility, rewards and recognition. If you do, you'll have a fantastic worker that is very loyal.

As for their preferences, abstract beauty appeals less to the native Taurus than concrete physical beauty, so objects and possessions purchased by the admiring Taurus will tend to have universal appeal. The Venus influence in a Taurus appreciates the beauty found in form a bit more than function.

The Earth Element and the Taurus Home

The earthy Taurus needs darker more sensual colors in the home to feel comfortable. Furniture and objects made of wood and stone offer physical earthly elements and, if crafted well, great beauty. Its best that objects made of these materials be carved and chiseled into solid whole structures from a solid whole piece, which is reflective of the solid stability of the native Taurus. Since the typical Taurus is very sensual, try to include luxurious textures like suede, fur and satin in your material choices. In general, there should be a feeling of calm, warmth and luxury surrounding you when you enter a Taurus home.

Taurus Colors

Dark Green
Dark Blue
Brown
Tan

Taurus Design Materials

Walnut
Cherry Wood
Natural Stone (with smooth texture)
Fur
Leather (Preferably textured)

The Taurus Living Room

In the main living areas, furniture pieces should be large and comfortable so that the hard-working Taurus can lounge around and enjoy the feeling of being relaxed. When you walk into a Taurus home, it should feel like a warm blanket that envelops you. Rich dark woods accompanied by seating that is fluffy and soft should be included. A great leather furniture piece can be used as an interesting accent in the living space.

Classic furniture in warm earth tones is featured in this living space. Accent pieces in rich leather and upholstered pieces with chenille add to the feel of luxury and comfort.

Don't worry too much about practicality when picking accents. The Taurus loves to have beautiful objects in the home regardless of their usefulness. In fact, if it's pleasant to the eye of the Taurus, then the object is considered useful. The floors should be smooth and even in color. A nice stone or dark wood floor would offer a solid base and be pleasant for a Taurus.

For a male Taurus, the ideal living space could resemble a British gentleman's club complete with large club chairs, stone or wood tables and a dark sophisticated atmosphere. For a woman, the style of a Mediterranean villa would offer the perfect design theme. Other preferred features in the Taurus living room would be sculptures, luxurious throws, a stone fireplace and crown molding.

The Taurus Kitchen and Dining Space

Gourmet food and cooking are very important to the native Taurus, so the kitchen needs to be large and have all of the necessary equipment needed to create a spectacular meal. However, the kitchen should not feel like a cold chef's kitchen. It needs to feel warm and cozy and have an area of entertainment where guests can watch the hard-working Taurus cook up a sumptuous feast.

Mediterranean features in this kitchen give it a warm feel. Note the expansive counter-top and bar area where guests can commune while in the kitchen area.

A large island with a seating area will allow guests to converse and mingle in the kitchen area while our diligent Taurus is cooking. Appliances should blend in as much as possible with the warmth of the cabinetry and counter-tops. A custom refrigerator dishwasher and/or trash compactor with façades that match the cabinetry would help keep the kitchen feeling inviting and uniform.

The dining area in the Taurus home should be a separate room complete with all of the luxurious extras. Place settings, formal wear, candles, chargers and a complete set of service wear are essential. The Taurus loves to eat their sumptuous meals in a beautifully decorated dining space. A great extra in the space would be a china cabinet that displays beautiful dinnerware collected over time.

The Taurus Bedroom

Like the living space, the Taurus bedroom must be comfortable and luxurious. Shades of blue, brown and tan are the ideal color scheme for the private resting space of the native bull. The room doesn't have to be very large; it just needs to feel cozy to meet the Taurus' needs. The room should also have plenty of daylight during the day. At night, lighting of a lower intensity would be preferred such as candlelight or sconce lighting.

Earthy and soothing colors are prominent in the bedroom. The comforter and pillows are of a satiny material and have a pleasant print with texture.

For the bed, satin sheets and plenty of bedding extras would be appreciated. If you want a Taurus to love their bedroom, deck it out and make it look like something out of a magazine. The Taurus enjoys looking at their beautiful bed as much as they enjoy sleeping in it. Add a super soft decorative rug or install a durable, but soft carpet to make it feel cozier. Add drapes to the window to both add beauty and provide darkness when resting.

The closet should be large or even a separate room as Taurus women and men tend to collect fine clothing and need a space to guard and display expensive pieces. Warm and solid wood such as walnut is ideal for the shelving and cabinetry in the Taurus closet. Add a bench at the foot of the bed and/or a comfortable chaise in the corner of the room as a nice statement piece.

The Taurus Bathroom

The most important element in the Taurus bathroom is the tub. It should be a large soaking tub, preferably one with jets. For the Taurus, smooth stone floors in the bathroom would be ideal. Dark wood cabinetry of a simple design works well in such a space and would add warmth that is uniform and sophisticated. The shower should be a good size and have a space where one can sit and relax.

The wood cabinetry, dark marble and the smooth stone floors complete the earthy look of this cozy bathroom.

The colors should be neutral and natural looking with accents of dark earthy greens or deep blues. If you want a great extra a Taurus would love, install radiant heat in the floors. Fluffy and luxurious towels should be a staple in the bathroom and can be displayed or tucked away in the cabinetry. Another great extra in a Taurus bathroom would be a well-crafted Sauna. The native Taurus would really enjoy detoxing in a room where they would be surrounded by heat and solid wood.

Chapter 3: The Gemini Home

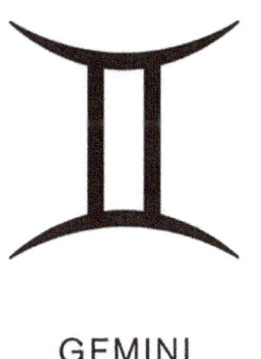

GEMINI

Gemini Description
Element: Air
Sign Quality: Mutable
Ruling Planet: Mercury
Zodiac House: Third House of Communication & Siblings
Corporeal Representation: Arms, Hands, Fingers & Shoulders

Gemini is the third sign of the Zodiac and those of this sun sign are characterized as highly communicative. Ruled by the communication planet, Mercury, Geminis are typically intellectual and analytical. They love to absorb new information and can get quite restless if they aren't exploring or learning something new. Books and communication gadgets are a staple in the Gemini home and it's not uncommon to find a television in almost every room.

The symbol for Gemini is "the twins", which describes the dual personality of the Gemini native. They tend to be very good at seeing both sides of an issue, yet this ability can also make it hard to know how a Gemini truly feels about something. Many may find a Gemini to be a bit illusive, evasive and fickle, but that is not the intention of the Gemini. They simply understand that most important issues are complicated and can readily identify with either side of any argument at any given moment.

The Air Element and the Gemini Home

The native Gemini is very comfortable talking and can talk quite a bit, so their home should be conducive to conversation and intellectual stimulation. As an air sign, the Gemini thrives on stimulation, so there should be interesting pieces in the home that serve as conversation starters. An off-beat piece of furniture or a decorative item with a great story behind it is certainly welcomed.

Try to stay away from dull and dark colors when decorating as most Geminis favor bright colors. The ideal color for the Gemini home is yellow as this color is bright, energetic and positive. Geometric patterns are also favored by intellectual Gemini, so it would be great to try to incorporate a geometric pattern in the décor.

Daylight and plenty of air is essential to creating a comfortable Gemini abode. There should be plenty of widows in the home, and if possible, an outdoor living space.

Indoor spaces that open up to outdoor spaces, which is common in the latest architectural trend of indoor/outdoor living, is ideal to the true Gemini.

Gemini Colors
Yellow
Lime Green
Peach
Pearly White

Gemini Design Materials
Hickory
Canary Wood
Silver
Plastics
Ceramics

The Gemini Living Room

The living room of a Gemini will likely be the most used space in the entire home. This space needs to have plenty of places to sit as the average Gemini has many friends and loves to have company. The television is likely to be the focal point, so it should be cutting edge technology. That way, the Gemini can have the pleasure of demonstrating and discussing the high-tech features of the television with their curious guests.

The largest piece in the living room should be a sectional sofa. It seats many, which comes in handy for the ultra-social Gemini. It would also be helpful if the coffee table doubles as a sitting space and has storage. If there is enough room, there should

Note the stimulating yellow accents against a neutral backdrop. The pillows are an iridescent taupe color and make a perfect quirky addition to a Gemini living space.

be extra chairs in the living area preferably chairs that are quirky and spark conversation.

Since Geminis tend to favor geometric patterns, try to incorporate patterns in the décor. An accent chair, rug or art piece with an interesting geometric pattern would suffice. Sculptures made of clay or carved from bright or light-colored materials like white marble or alabaster are great decorative statements as well.

Reading materials are both an accessory and a source of entertainment for the native Gemini, so there should be plenty of books and magazines in the living room. If possible, a small area of the living space can be used as a library. What would be ideal for a Gemini is to have a separate library room adjacent to the living room so that any topic of conversation can be followed up on or investigated further with books in the library.

The Gemini Kitchen and Dining Area

The kitchen space should be large enough for multiple cooks. Most Gemini natives love to share the labor of making a meal as it gives them the opportunity to converse and share ideas while cooking. Stainless steel counter tops work great in the Gemini kitchen due to the stimulating quality of a reflective metal surface. Add a

This kitchen space is large and expansive with stainless steel appliances and hardware. The colors are neutral, but the lighting and unique counter-tops add interest.

backsplash with an interesting geometric pattern to make a great feature and provide more stimuli. As a great extra, try to include a space designated for books on cooking and exotic foods that the native Gemini can refer to often while creating a meal.

The dining space is also an area of the Gemini home where lively conversations would take place. Chairs in this area should be comfortable so that guests can sit and talk for hours if caught up in a lively discussion. The area should be well lit so that any items like books or interesting objects brought into the room can be seen by all of the guests. Some Gemini natives may favor having a television in the dining space to keep up with the latest in entertainment and news while enjoying a meal.

The Gemini Bedroom

A TV Lift would be a fun and useful addition to the Gemini Bedroom.

Generally, a bedroom is a place where you rest and rejuvenate and this is no exception for the native Gemini. However, there still must be sources of communication in a Gemini bedroom for them to feel the most comfortable. Although generally not recommended, the Gemini is the only sign for whom you could consider putting a TV in the bedroom. The only clause is that the TV must be in an apparatus where it can be covered and hidden out of sight when it's time to sleep. A clever mechanical TV lift that can be installed at the foot of the bed would be ideal and provide conversation piece as well.

As for the color scheme, a Gemini does best in rooms with a pastel pallet. Peach, pale yellow and lavender would work well in a female's room and mauve or taupe would be good for a male's room. These colors are still stimulating, but are more relaxed. Furniture pieces should be of a light-colored wood. Dark colors are not recommended for Gemini, so where possible, wood tones like Beechwood, birch or oak

Pale yellow is a soothing color, yet is energetic enough for a Gemini bedroom. Men might want to use shades of taupe and grey for a more masculine look.

would be ideal. The nightstand needs to have storage space where books and magazines can be stashed for nighttime reading. If there is enough space, a reading nook complete with a comfortable chair and lighting can be incorporated in the bedroom.

The Gemini Bathroom

Like the Aries, the Gemini native will not spend as much time in the bathroom, so this space doesn't need to be very large or decked out. It does, however, need to have the latest in technology. A mirror with a built-in TV monitor would be excellent for a Gemini and allow them to catch up on the latest news while getting ready in the morning. A morning dose of information would get a true Gemini pumped and ready to face the day.

The light-colored wood of the sink area is ideal for the Gemini. The space is simple and offers the necessities, which is perfect for the busy Gemini. You can see that daylight filters through to the shower area.

If at all possible, the bathroom should get plenty of daylight and be well ventilated. It is recommended that a Gemini have a window in the bathroom that can be opened to let in fresh air. The Gemini native would be very uncomfortable in a bathroom that is too dark and has no windows. The ideal scenario would include a sliding door that opens up to a private outdoor space off of the bathroom.

The color scheme can mirror that of the bedroom, incorporating lighter pastel colors. Pair these colors with neutrals, like beige, tan or a light grey to keep with the theme of relaxation in the bathroom. A great added design feature in a Gemini bathroom would be iridescent or pearly white accents. The Gemini finds pearly or iridescent elements energizing.

Chapter 4: The Cancer Home

CANCER

Cancer Description
Element: Water
Sign Quality: Cardinal
Ruling Planet: The Moon
Zodiac House: Fourth House of Home & Family
Corporeal Representation: Chest, Breasts, Digestive System, Womb & Pancreas

Cancer is the fourth sign of the zodiac and people of this sun sign are known to be family oriented and prefer stability in the home environment. Cancers aren't typically prone to wandering or changing their residence very often, so having a comfortable and beautiful home is ultra-important. As a Water sign, Cancers are very much in touch with their feelings. In fact, they tend to be highly intuitive sensing any negative or positive emotion coming from others. For this reason, it is important for the Native Cancer to have an environment that is protective and filled with positive energy.

Represented by "the Crab", a true Cancer is very reclusive, choosing only a select few people into their private lives. Even though the Cancer is a water sign that likes to go with the flow of their emotions, they are also a Cardinal sign and it shows in their ability to create and stabilize a healthy home environment. If you are looking for someone to start a solid family structure with, you would do well to partner up with a Cancer.

The Water Element and the Cancer Home

The water element gives the Cancer highly intuitive nature so they don't need to speak much or even converse to communicate. If you're lucky enough to have a Cancer invite you into their home and find them very quiet, don't think of it as an insult. Cancers can almost feel your emotions and empathize well, but they don't verbalize this fact due to their crab-like need to remain in their shells.

Due to the watery and emotional nature of the Cancer, you will find that they have a very comfortable home filled with everything they need. The water element makes the native Cancer very nurturing, so you'll find lots of extras in the home to make guests and family members feel comfortable. Extra throw blankets and pillows can be found in every room of the Cancer home.

Cancers love daylight, but also enjoy darkness. The daylight for the Cancer is a source of energy and revitalization and darkness provides an environment for introspection and recuperation. There should be plenty of windows, but they must have quality coverings that can block the light out completely when needed.

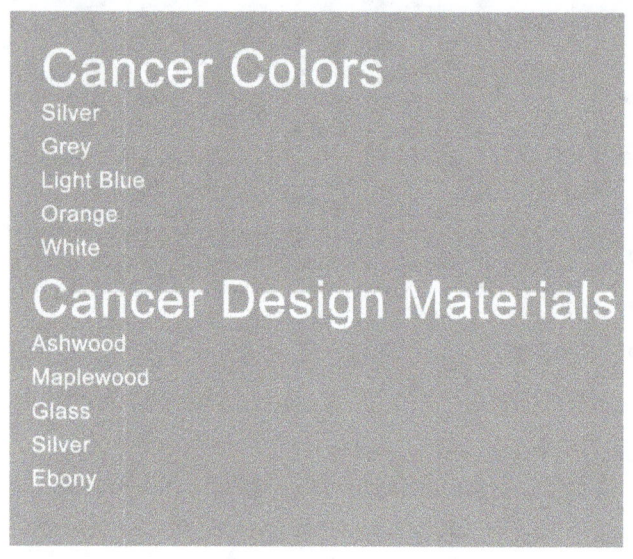

Cancer Colors
Silver
Grey
Light Blue
Orange
White

Cancer Design Materials
Ashwood
Maplewood
Glass
Silver
Ebony

The Cancer Living Room

The Cancer living space should feel warm, inviting and spacious enough to accommodate their immediate and extended family. A sofa/loveseat combination or large oversized sectional would be idea and should be made of a natural fiber like cotton or linen. Pops of orange would work to add energy to the space and increase positive feelings. Silvery blue also works well, but provides a more calming energy. Orange and blue are complementary colors, so having plenty of throw pillows in both colors would be perfect. Oversized chairs and plenty of

Orange is an energetic color and can bring an element of energy and positive feelings to the living space. Natural fibers would be preferred by the native Cancer and would give a warm feel to the space.

throw blankets should be around as well for family members that stop by.

A Cancer doesn't necessarily need a TV, but if one is needed it should be placed so as not to transfer noise to other adjacent rooms, particularly any adjacent bedrooms. Peace and quiet is important to most Cancers, and general TV noise can be quite annoying to a Cancer. Conversely, the noise of children at play and family conversations are very comforting. In general, make sure the living room is the area that is most attractive for lingering family and guest. That way, when the native Cancer needs time alone they can sneak away in peace and quiet.

The Cancer Kitchen and Dining Area

The sign of Cancer rules the digestive system; hence cooking food is very important to a Cancer native. You will find that most Cancers are intuitively good at cooking. After all, Cancer is the sign of nurturing and feeding themselves and the family is the ultimate display of their nurturing instinct. As such, the kitchen should be large and have every appliance available to create a fantastic home cooked meal. Even for Cancers that don't cook, a great kitchen is essential. After all, mom may stop by and make a meal.

A pot rack would be very useful and add a fun design element in the Cancer kitchen. It also makes it easy for the native Cancer to access pots and not worry about having to neatly stash them away.

Copper colors are great for a Cancer kitchen. A nice pot rack with copper pots makes a great design feature and stores pots out of reach of children. The stove should be a gourmet gas stove in stainless steel. Decorative baskets filled with ready-to-eat fruits make a beautiful and useful accessory to have in the kitchen as well. Cancers are less concerned about tidiness than most signs, so kitchen appliances don't necessarily need to be stored. A great way to keep the design element of a Cancer kitchen without making it look too busy is to color coordinate the counter-top appliances. They are likely to remain out in the open.

The dining space should be large and have ample seating. Even a single Cancer may feel the need to have a grand dining space in case family comes by for dinner.

Warm wood tones and soft fabrics would be welcomed in a Cancer dining space. A great extra feature would be monogramed slip-covers. Cancers would be very attached to the family name and history and would love a detail like this in the space where the family would gather to share a meal.

Natural wood tables are favored by the Cancer as the wood gives a warm feel to the dining space and is durable. Chairs should be slip-covered for easy cleaning since it's likely that the native Cancer has children of their own or will have them visit often.

Most Cancers are not as concerned about having all of the formal dining accoutrements. They are more concerned that there is enough dinnerware for all of the guests. There should be multiple dinnerware sets of the same style to ensure that everyone can be accommodated.

The Cancer Bedroom

The bedroom is one of the most important spaces in the home of the Cancer. It is the space where a Cancer is most likely to retreat when they need to escape the world and recuperate. It is essential that this space be very quiet. If it is an option, a Cancer should consider sound proofing the bedroom if it is near areas of the home with more traffic and noise.

Shades of grey, silver and burnt orange are the ideal colors for the Cancer bedroom. A nice light or silvery blue would suffice as well. Bedding should be luxurious and soft to the skin. Use only natural fiber sheets such as cotton and make sure they have a high thread count. Windows should have heavy drapes that completely block out the sun when needed. Overall, there should be nothing to stir up too much excitement in this room. It should be relaxing, subdued and conducive to quiet time and intimacy with their mate.

This room has a good amount of sunlight and offers plantation shades that block out the light when needed. The sofa at the foot of the bed would make a great lounge area where the Cancer can retreat and read or simply be alone when needed. Warm wood tones also help this room feel cozy and inviting.

Cancers grow attached to sentimental items, like old gifts and clothes that trigger nostalgia. Hence, the closet should be large and well organized so that they can easily access treasured keepsakes. Since the native Cancer is not a stickler for order, the design of the closet space should be focused on order to make it easy for the Cancer to keep it up. It is recommended that a space organizer or closet design specialist be consulted to ensure ease of access and organization.

The Cancer Bathroom

Cancers of either gender will tend to spend a lot of time in the bathroom, particularly in the bathtub. Baths are soothing and rejuvenating for both Cancer females and males. Therefore, the bathtub can be the focal point. The bathtub should be large, beautiful and enable a Cancer native to submerge completely in the water. Jets may not be needed as this may be too much stimulation for most Cancers looking to relax in

A glass enclosed shower and a separate tub with a rich wood base are the standout features in this tranquil bathroom. The tub is very large and will allow a watery Cancer to be completely immersed.

tranquility.

White, silvery grey, beige or light blue is the ideal color palette for the bathroom. Glass tiles are also a preferred feature and can add a great design element to the shower or walls. Unlike the native Gemini, a Cancer does not need much sunlight in the bathroom. In fact, candlelight would be preferred. A steam room and towel warmers would be a fantastic extra for the Cancer bathroom.

Chapter 5: The Leo Home

LEO

> ## Leo Description
> **Element:** Fire
> **Sign Quality:** Fixed
> **Ruling Planet:** The Sun
> **Zodiac House:** Fifth House of Fun, Romance & Speculation
> **Corporeal Representation:** Heart, Spine, Upper Back & Spleen

Leo is the fifth sign of the zodiac and these people are typically characterized as romantic, grandiose, affectionate, larger-than-life and very generous. The Leo craves the spotlight and it certainly seems to find them. In fact, you will find that many celebrities and members of royalty have Leo as a sun, ascendant sign or on the cusp of the fourth house.

Leos will gladly enter any competition as long as the play is fair for they are not sore losers and can appreciate being defeated by a skilled opponent. Defeat, after all, is how they learn. Leos are also gamblers and thrive on risk taking. They are willing to take a risk to get what they want and aren't easily discouraged by failure, which gives them the power of wish fulfilment.

The ego is also very important to a typical Leo as their ruling planet, the sun, is the zodiac's representation of the ego drive. As a fixed sign, Leos can have a stubborn streak to them. Once they get moving in a certain direction, it can be rather difficult for them to change course. Some Leos can be so intent on getting their way, they can continue stubbornly on the wrong path just to prove their will power.

The Fire Element and the Leo Home

The Leo home can best be described as a palace. The native Leo loves drama and opulence in the home. It is not uncommon for the Leo home to be a mecca for grand parties and gatherings of the who's who in the neighborhood. When you enter a Leo home you can expect to find bright colors, music, fun and games.

The fire element is very active and consuming, so the Leo home must have activity at all times, whether the Leo is taking part in the activity or not. You will find any guest rooms very comfortable grand and filled with all of the essentials. Common features of the fiery Leo's home would be fireplaces and outdoor fire pits. Precious works of art or a self-portrait are likely to be found in the home of a true Leo as well.

Leo Colors
Gold
Bright Yellow
Red-Orange
Orange
White

Leo Design Materials
Mahogany
Cedar
Gold
Velvet
Exotic Furs

The Leo Living Room

Ideally, the Leo home would have both a formal living room and a family room. The formal living space should have very elegant furniture with classic embellishments. It should be rather quiet, but have a strong presence as it will be the place where any important guests will be received. Jacquard prints, furs, and tapestries are great design elements for the Leo formal living space.

The less formal family room should be very comfortable and fun. It is likely that this room will have the latest entertainment gadgets for less formal gatherings and parties. A large TV, the latest video gaming console and a centralized audio system would suit a Leo family room very well and get a lot of use. Bright yellow and gold are great colors for the family room as

Note the gold accents in this opulent formal living space. The high ceilings give it a grand look and the classic styling of the furniture evokes a palatial feel.

these colors represent warmth and generosity, which is much like the Leo personality.

The furniture should be large and very comfortable. Leos love to be showy, so any pillows or throws should be high quality and offer the feel of luxury. A classic oriental or animal skin rug would work perfectly as a compliment to the luxurious seating. Any cabinetry or storage in the living space should be mahogany or any other type of sturdy high-quality wood.

The Leo Kitchen and Dining Area

Leos love grand meals and gourmet cooking. Therefore, the kitchen should be fully stocked with everything one would need to create a five-star meal. It is likely that the Leo would have a maid or cook if they can afford it, so a room off of the kitchen with all of the comforts a maid would need would be recommended. Leos are very generous, so the maid's quarters would likely be very beautiful and comfortable.

Cabinetry in the kitchen should be of a dark wood as this gives the kitchen a royal and opulent feel. Floors can be wood or a luxurious stone such as marble. Highly polished brass is another great feature for a Leo kitchen as brass resembles gold. Adding brass fixtures and hardware would help complete the look.

This dining space has very classic style and is complete with opulent embellishments. It seats many and offers space and comfort for the dinner guests of the generous Leo.

As for the dining space, the Leo would likely prefer to have both a breakfast dining area and a formal dining room. The breakfast area should get plenty of daylight or be situated outside. It is an area where a Leo would eat a quick meal, sip an afternoon cup of coffee or tea, or simply lounge and read the paper.

In the formal dining room, the table must be very large and seat many people with plenty of elbow room. Chairs can be leather or upholstered with an embellished fabric. Gold flatware and plates with gold rims are ideal for the Leo formal dining room as well. There should be the full array of service equipment and trays so that all meals can be properly served. Rugs aren't typically recommended for the dining area, but for the Leo, a large luxurious rug would offer the grand look they love.

The Leo Bedroom

Comfort and beauty should be the main themes in a Leo bedroom. The bed is likely the most important focal point, so it should be fluffy and grand with many decorative pillows. Shades of gold and white would make a revitalizing space for the royal Leo. Warm, yet light, earth tones like tan, grey or mint green can be used for a calming effect.

In this 3D rendering, gold accents and luxurious fabrics characterize the ideal bedroom of the average Leo. Both males and females would find this room luxurious.

Accessories can include a soft and fluffy rug and luxurious drapes. Leos typically love embellishments and well-crafted furniture pieces, so a well-crafted dresser and/or bench would make a welcome addition in the bedroom. The room should get plenty of sunlight as well. Leos are ruled by the sun and find sunlight revitalizing. The native Leo is one of the few signs that can sleep soundly in a room filled with bright sunlight.

The Leo closet should be a large walk-in space and have ample room for jewelry as most Leos love accessories. In fact, there should be more of a focus on organizing accessories than clothing as a Leo will value changing their look with different accessories over buying new outfits. Leos love themes for their closets. For a Leo male, a gentleman's club or cigar room theme would be perfect. A glamorous palace theme complete with a sparkling chandelier would be ideal for a Leo female's closet space.

The Leo Bathroom

Luxurious stone and opulent finishes are the epitome of Leo style. Note the golden print on the walls and the vanity.

This is the space in a Leo home where they get ready to wow their adoring fans, so emphasis should be put on a very accommodating vanity area. For a female, there should be plenty of room for make-up and hair accessories as most Leos have quite a "mane" of hair. Leo men also tend to have great heads of hair and they take the care and maintenance of it very seriously.

Like the Cancer, Leos love to bathe, but they are more likely to share the experience with a mate than a Cancer, so the tub should accommodate two. The invigoration of a whirlpool or Jacuzzi jets are also preferred by the native Leo when bathing, so if possible, try to include jets in the tub. Like the tub, the shower needs to be invigorating. Ideally, the shower area would be large and have multiple shower heads and sprays.

Chapter 6: The Virgo Home

VIRGO

Virgo Description
Element: Earth
Sign Quality: Mutable
Ruling Planet: Mercury
Zodiac House: Sixth House of Health, Service & Daily Routine
Corporeal Representation: The Nervous System

Virgo is the sixth sign of the Zodiac and people of this sun sign are known to be analytical, observant and focused on health. Ruled by Mercury, the planet of communication, Virgos are very good at expressing themselves and communicating complicated subjects. They are also adept at learning languages and will typically speak more than one. They also make great lawyers due to their analytical and communication skills.

Virgos tend to love taking the reins in organizing events and/or reorganizing a space. If you need someone to help you get your life in order or help you organize your finances, a great Virgo friend would be ideal. They are generally non-judgmental when you come to them for help and focus only of discovering the problem and fixing it.

Virgos absolutely need to have a clean and tidy space in order to function properly. You can visibly observe the discomfort on the face of the true Virgo when in a messy space. Health is also of great concern to the Virgo, so you'll find that exercise and good eating habits come up often as topics of conversation.

The Earth Element and the Virgo Home

As an earth sign, Virgo tends to focus on practical day-to-day life, so the home will generally be neat and in order. You will find a general theme of cleanliness and health as well. Organizational systems appeal to the native Virgo, so you may find that many things are labeled and/or placed in some kind of sequence.

There should be a very marked sense of practicality in the design and decoration of the Virgo home. It is important that almost every object in the Virgo home have some kind of useful purpose. Earthy elements in the home appeal to the native Virgo as they help provide a sense of comfort. You'll find plenty of natural materials and plants in the home of a true Virgo.

Virgo Colors
Brown
Tan
Green
Grey
White

Virgo Design Materials
Beechwood
Zebra Wood
Linen
Cotton
Concrete

The Virgo Living Room

The living space of the native Virgo should be modern and sophisticated, yet uncluttered and minimalist. A Virgo would likely appreciate the minimalist and practical designs of Architect Tadao Ando, who is also a Virgo himself. Every piece of furniture in a Virgo's living room should have a practical purpose as true Virgos prefer order over prestige.

A simple sofa or sectional in white or a warm and earthy hue would be preferred. A straight-forward coffee table with clean lines would make a great compliment to the sofa. If the table has multiple practical uses, that would also be ideal to a Virgo. For example, a coffee table that offers use as a serving area and/or storage space.

Furniture with simple design and clean lines is featured in this modern living room. Every piece has a specific purpose and any decorative items are simple.

Like Gemini, the Virgo loves to learn new information. They are simply better at communicating that information and assimilating it into practical application than most signs. As such, the living space should have room for books and magazines. As a side note: Virgos really appreciate educational books more than fiction, so a national geographic subscription or a book on architecture or art would be a perfect gift for a Virgo friend. Virgo's like entertainment, so a large TV with very high definition would be great. They would take great pleasure in being able to see every detail of an educational show on Animal Planet, TLC or National Geographic.

The Virgo Kitchen and Dining Area

This modern kitchen with neutral colors and plenty of storage is practical and simple.

Like the living space, the kitchen area must be neat and organized. Virgos do appreciate cooking and serving those they love, so the kitchen will need to have everything needed to make a great meal. Virgos can't stand it when they do not have the right tool for the right job, so they will need lots of storage space for the many counter-top appliances and cookware they'll need. Cluttered counter-tops are a no-no for the highly organized Virgo.

Colors in the Virgo kitchen should be neutral and monochromatic. Bold colors affect the native Virgo's concentration, so shades of grey or beige will do for this space. Virgos typically have a great attention span and need an environment that helps them to concentrate when doing any kind of work. If you want to add more interest in the kitchen area, incorporate sophisticated elements such as stainless steel or decorative tile in a neutral color.

It is fulfilling for a Virgo to cook and serve a fantastic meal for friends, so the dining space needs to have enough space for many guests. However, the minimalist and clean style should be continued. The table should be large and neutral. A simple concrete top dining table and simple well-constructed chairs would make the perfect set-up for a Virgo dining space. Benches as opposed to chairs would work as well and make for an even less cluttered look.

The Virgo Bedroom

Peace and serenity should characterize the Virgo bedroom. Soft neutrals and whites are ideal. The bed does not need to be decked out in pillows as Virgos prefer the bed to be practical, clean and ready to use. For Virgo females, pillows that are both beautiful and useful as backrests for bedtime reading would suffice. For the Virgo male, have a simple set of pillows that are orthopedic for sleep and a couple of extra pillows.

This rendering shows a modern style bedroom with simple bedding and plenty of storage space where the tidy Virgo can store personal items.

Like the Gemini, lighting near the bed for reading is highly recommended. However, a separate reading space or reading nook is not necessary as it may make the room feel too crowded. If you need to have added furniture, it should be a dresser of simple design where extra clothing and bedding can be stored.

The Virgo closet would generally be very organized and may even have labels. Every item a Virgo owns as far as clothing, shoes and accessories go, needs to have its designated place. The Virgo is typically very good at organizing their own space, so the closet should have ample shelving so that the native Virgo can add their own organizational system to the space. Make sure that the closet is very well lit. The Virgo wants to see what they have to wear and quickly and efficiently put an outfit together.

The Virgo Bathroom

For the Virgo, the bathroom space is meant for cleaning the body and maintaining health. Baths aren't as frequent for a Virgo, but a very powerful and hot shower is like heaven to them. For the native Virgo, a shower ensures that any dirt is washed off of the body and down the drain for good.

The large shower is the main feature in this simple, yet elegant bathroom. Note the neutral color pallet and dark wood cabinetry.

As such, the shower should be the largest area of the bathroom. Plenty of spray jets in multiple positions would be ideal. If the shower space can double as a steam room, that would be even better. A Virgo would appreciate sweating out impurities in a steam room and washing them away with a great shower.

Towels should be white as the Virgo wants to be aware of how clean they are. There should be a storage area to hide towels and a bin where dirty towels can be placed. A typical Virgo will go through many hand and body towels, so there should be ample supply.

A large mirror is recommended as well as a magnifying mirror so that the Virgo can see details when grooming. Ventilation is also very important for a Virgo in the bathroom. A window that can be opened would be preferred. However, if that isn't an option, a powerful but quiet fan should be installed.

Chapter 7: **The Libra Home**

LIBRA

> **Libra Description**
> **Element:** Air
> **Sign Quality:** Cardinal
> **Ruling Planet:** Venus
> **Zodiac House:** Seventh House of Partnership & Marriage
> **Corporeal Representation:** Lower Back, Kidneys & Adrenal Glands

Libra is the seventh sign in the Zodiac and Libra natives are known to be diplomatic, peacemaking, social and intellectual. Libras are usually very cerebral, yet possess a gift for being pleasantly engaging. They seem to know just what to say and just what to do in any given social situation. Ruled by the planet Venus, Libras can be very romantic and love to express themselves with beauty, whether it be in style of dress or art.

Represented by the scales, the Libra loves to balance things and thrives in a partnership. Libras can see both sides of an argument very clearly, which can make them quite indecisive at times. It is said to be the most frustrating characteristic of the sign. However, the Libra can have the ability to make firm decisions when in partnership because they have to accommodate "the other". If you want an understanding partner that will help you see both sides of an issue with tact and patience, then a Libra is ideal for you.

The Air Element and the Libra Home

Balanced is the word that should come to mind when describing the ideal Libran home. They are likely to have a great selection of pieces that reflect both great style and practicality. The air element enables them to appreciate a friendly intellectual debate and they appreciate learning something new from other intelligent individuals, so the Libra home should be a place where comfortable conversation can take place.

The air element influence on the native Libra makes them crave open spaces. As such, natural light, high ceilings and large windows appeal greatly to them. A great feature for a Libra home would be skylights, particularly ones that can open and let in fresh air.

Libran décor typically gravitates towards a basic Asian theme. This kind of style appeals to the Libra because they favor simplicity and overall harmony, which is central to Asian décor. Also, the theme provides a great anchor to guide the, sometimes indecisive, Libra when choosing items. The intellectual and changeable nature of the Libra can also lead them to prefer an eclectic style of décor, so you may find varied styles featured. A Libra is one of the only signs that can pull off great eclectic style.

Libra Colors
Pink
Pale Green
Pale Blue
Salmon
Black

Libra Design Materials
Pine
Bamboo
Ebony
Copper
Ceramics

The Libra Living Room

The living space of the Libra should have a comfortable sitting space that is beautiful, but is not too large. Libras love company, but they do not like too many people in the home. A small intimate gathering of friends makes it easier for the group to have a fruitful conversation. An area rug that defines the space and is soft enough to sit on would work well in this area. Large

The color scheme in this living space is very basic but provides contrast, which appeals to the Libra. The space is expansive and has large windows to let in air and light.

pillows to sit on are also a great extra.

Colors need to be calming, but offer stimulation through contrast. A color scheme of black and white would appeal to most Libras, salmon and pale green may be favored by females. Décor pieces should provide exposure to all of the elements. For example: a small decorative fountain to represent water, ceramic vases to represent earth, high ceilings and open windows for plenty of air circulation and a fire place would provide a balanced environment.

Like fellow air signs Gemini and Aquarius, the Libra loves information and discussion, so there should be pieces in the living area that can help strike up interesting conversation. An artifact from travels or an off-beat coffee table book would do well. Libras aren't big on watching TV, so it may not be necessary to have one in the living space. A radio, however, may be preferred and very stimulating for the Libra native. Libras love almost all types of music and can listen to a radio for hours. Radio news programs are also much liked by many Libran individuals.

The Libra Kitchen and Dining Area

There is a high degree of contrast in this modern kitchen. Rich wood with a notable wood grain against a stark white backdrop provides the balance that the Libra craves. Note that a few select items are on display such as a specialty coffee maker and a tea pot.

The kitchen is simply another living space for the Libra. Conversations would easily travel from the living space to the kitchen when guests get hungry. Therefore, the open concept living, kitchen and dining area are recommended for the Libran home. Such a layout would be great for keeping a conversation going between the living and kitchen area.

The kitchen should be organized and offer visually pleasing cooking elements displayed in a balanced and decorative way. A beautiful teapot on the stove or rack of shiny and reflective pots on display works great. Counter tops should be smooth and even. A quartz counter top would be ideal as this offers a solid surface in one solid color. This will allow the Libra to decorate with items that contrast with the counter top.

An underlying eastern theme can continue in the dining room as well if that is the direction chosen by the Libra. A low wood table with soft floor pillows makes for a comfortable eating space that is relaxed and conducive to conversation. You are highly likely to find cookware and service items for exotic foods as well. A full set of chopsticks, a tagine or an alternative device for making coffees and teas might all be on display.

For the Libra that prefers a more western dining set-up, the table should be a contrasting color or texture from the chairs and/or walls. Libras strive for balance, so playing with opposite colors on the color wheel is recommended. Since Libras typically love food from all over the world and are more likely to eat exotic eastern foods more often than not; decorative flatware, plates and service utensils can vary widely. For instance, Asian, Thai or Indian themed eatery would be beautiful and practical.

The Libra Bedroom

The typical Libra needs silence a bit more than other air signs, so the bedroom needs to be conducive to rest, relaxation and calm. Soothing pale shades of blue, grey and/or green would help the true Libra to enter a calm and reflective state of mind. The bed can be simple and offer a bit of contrast by using whites against blacks or a pale blue against a pale orange or plain white.

The bedroom is more for rest than intellectual pursuits for most Libras, so the lighting can be low and soothing in this space. The Libra functions well with a bed close to the floor, which is in line with an eastern or Asian theme. Furniture should be minimal, but offer beauty and style. Great accessories in a Libran bedroom can be a kimono, a simple dresser or a lovely rug with an interesting pattern.

A platform bed with simple style is great for the native Libra. These beds are usually lower to the ground, which is beneficial to the Libran. The accessories are low key, but add interest in the space.

The closet area for a Libra should have a lot of storage since Libras love to dress well. They shop very often and can collect clothing items of various styles. Therefore, the closet should help them to organize by style and even occasion. Libras go out a lot due to their pleasant and social nature, so they need to be able to quickly gather an outfit from among their large collections of clothing, shoes and accessories.

The closet should be well lit and well ventilated as Libras love fresh air and a walk-in closet space can be a bit stuffy if not designed correctly. If there is a window in the closet, excellent! Better yet, if the Libra native can afford it, they should have a separate room as a closet space and get it professionally organized.

The Libra Bathroom

A Zen-like Asian spa is the ideal theme for the Libra bathroom. A light stone floor with bamboo wood accents would work well and be beautiful. Libras love to both bathe and shower and can spend a considerable amount of time doing both. Therefore, both the bathtub and the shower should be prominent. If possible, having a separate shower and tub area would be perfect.

This Zen-like bathroom is ideal for Librans. This bathroom offers the contrast of wood against white, lots of space and plenty of daylight.

Like the Leo, the Libra certainly needs a vanity area to get ready. However, it does not need to be as large as it would be for a Leo. Libras are efficient when grooming and like to keep it simple. A sitting area with a mirror and a small attached cabinet for supplies would suffice. Ventilation is also very important to a Libra in the bathroom. A bathroom that has a wide view of a private outdoor garden would be ideal and add serenity. A great extra that a Libra would appreciate is a detached sauna. They won't spend too much time in it, but they would use it very often and would likely enjoy the wood and fire element to contrast with the watery theme of the bathroom.

Chapter 8: The Scorpio Home

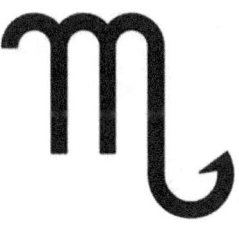

SCORPIUS

Scorpio Description
Element: Water
Sign Quality: Fixed
Ruling Planet: Pluto
Zodiac House: Eighth House of Intimacy & Shared Resourses
Corporeal Representation: Genitals, Bladder & Urinary Tract

Scorpio represents the eighth house of the Zodiac and is known to be the most passionate and intense sign. Ruled by Pluto, the planet of life, death, sex, secrets, intense passion and obsession; Scorpios are powerfully intuitive and possess an innate understanding of human nature. They tend to be very private and are highly astute, often noticing details and behaviors that others may miss. They are very loyal lovers and friends where their intensity can be, at times, overwhelming.

They make fantastic allies as they are very loyal, but they make very scary enemies due to an almost uncontrollable need for revenge. Conversely, some Scorpios have a tremendous gift for self-mastery that usually comes with age. In fact, time is a friend of the native Scorpio. Many find older Scorpios very mature, sexy, intuitive and wise.

Since the eight house deals with sex, it's a part of life that Scorpios tend to naturally understand. Not so much the act itself, but the intensity of mutual sharing, so many can have a preoccupation with emotional intimacy. The eight houses also rules other people's things, so Scorpios are generally respectful of other people's property and can sometimes handle a partner's possessions and finances better than their own.

The Water Element and the Scorpio Home

When it comes to the home, the Scorpio likes to express their intensity in hidden and creative ways. As a water sign, they are quite deep and want their living space to allow deep introspection. Letting the emotions flow freely is essential to a Scorpio when in their private space since they tend to hide their intensity in public.

You may find that the Scorpio home feels like a secret cave. It will likely be rather dark and warm, but not in a somber way. Too much sunlight and large open windows would not be the ideal features for a Scorpio home. Dark, sultry and sensual is what you should look for when designing the Scorpio abode. If you need inspiration when designing a Scorpio's home, think of the depths of the ocean where it's dark and mysterious, but also where great beauty can be found. If you want to really please a Scorpio, add a secret room or incorporate a secret passage way in the design scheme. The planet Pluto rules Scorpio and Pluto appreciates secret and hidden places.

Scorpio Colors
Purple
Maroon
Burgundy
Magenta
Black

Scorpio Design Materials
Teak
Iron
Moroccan Prints
Silk
Ceramics

The Scorpio Living Room

The living room of a Scorpio home is a very private space for them. It should feel like an exotic secret room where only trusted and loyal friends can gather. As such, dark and rich colors should be used. Middle Eastern and Moroccan décor and color schemes appeal the most to the Scorpio. Spanish style and décor also has an appeal due to the Moroccan influence in Spanish design.

Rich dark wood furniture paired with reds and tans make this space cozy and inviting. The room is dark and has lots of plant life, which Scorpios appreciate.

A sitting area on the floor with beautiful pillows and a decorative rug would be ideal. Heavy drapes with intricate embellishments also fit the Scorpio living space. Black-out drapes should be considered as well to keep the space dark and intimate when needed. Candlelight is usually favored by the Scorpio as bright lighting is disturbing. Daylight is appreciated when the Scorpio is outside with their inner nature safely tucked away in their Scorpio shell. However, in the home, sensual low lighting is the way to go.

Water is comforting to the Scorpio, so a decorative fountain in the living area would provide interest and the soothing sound of flowing water. Plants are appreciated as well. Even though their space is typically dark, you can incorporate plants like Monestera or Calathea, which are exotic plants that grow in more shaded areas.

The Scorpio Kitchen and Dining Area

Scorpios typically love the intense flavors of foods from the East, so you'll typically smell exotic spices emanating from the kitchen. The colors in the kitchen should be dark brown from natural woods with pops if maroon or dark red, perhaps incorporated in an exotic print tile on the backsplash.

The look of the kitchen should be almost primitive with basic terracotta floors and wooden spice racks with all of the flavors of Indian and Moroccan cuisine. A nice window over the kitchen sink with a view of a private garden would work well as ventilation and daylight to illuminate the space. In fact, the kitchen would likely be

Exotic spices are typically a staple in the Scorpio kitchen. You can take color cues from a spice market when designing a Scorpio's home.

the brightest space in a Scorpio home.

As suggested for the living space, a nice low table with beautiful floor pillows would work great in the dining area. Otherwise, a sturdy dark wood table and beautifully embellished chairs would work

Modern design with rustic features would make a great kitchen for the native Scorpio. In this case, rough wood cabinet doors and drawers are the rustic element.

well. Add decorative cushions to the chairs to add comfort and complete the look. Place settings, plates and flatware should reflect an Asian or Middle-Eastern theme to complement the overall style of the space. Scorpios like to hide things, so a beautifully embellished cabinet where dining supplies can be stashed away would be ideal.

The Scorpio Bedroom

The ideal bedroom for a Scorpio would feel like a cocoon; a place where the sensitive Scorpio can relax, recover and emerge anew. Intimacy is also very important to the Scorpio, so sensual colors, smells and lighting is essential in this space. Candlelight, incense, and a luxurious bed are perfect.

The bed should have many pillows and double as a place to sleep and a place to lounge and engage in intimate conversation. It is recommended that the bed be large so much time can be spent comfortably by two or more people. Scorpio women will usually commune with loyal male and female friends on the bed chatting for hours. Scorpio males tend to do work in the bed and typically have close female and male platonic relationships, so they will also use the bed as a lounge and conversation space.

The closet space can vary for Scorpios. Some collect many items only to purge them a year or two later and some will have the ability to go with very little clothing, only

A canopy bed is great for the Scorpio native. They would love the feeling of being enclosed in the bed area. The bed is king sized and has shades of magenta, a preferred color for many female Scorpios.

possessing what is essentials to them. Such is the nature of a sign ruled by Pluto, which loves to purge and start anew or focus only on what is absolutely necessary.

Either way, organization of this area is important. It can be a large walk-in closet or a small one, but everything must be visible. Although Scorpios love to hide things, it is a different story when it comes to getting dressed. They must see all of the options available to make a decision on what to wear for the day. Open shelving and cubby holes for shoes work well as they allow everything to be seen, but also stay organized.

The Scorpio Bathroom

The bathroom is perhaps the most important area in a Scorpio's home. The bathroom is ruled by Pluto as it is a place where we purge waste and clean our bodies. The Scorpio bathroom should be a sanctuary where the Scorpio can become clean in privacy. The key word is privacy as a Scorpio is not comfortable sharing a bathroom with anyone. Only very close friends and their mate are allowed to enter this space, so if possible, there should be a separate guest bathroom for any visitors.

A large bathtub is very much appreciated by the Scorpio. The rustic look of the brick and the low lighting make this an ideal space for the Scorpio native to relax and recuperate.

The Scorpio can spend much time in the bathroom because they love to bathe, much like the native Cancer and Pisces. The tub should be large and allow for total immersion. The bathroom should also have low light and/or no windows, unless, the windows open up to a private space where no one can ever see into the space. A great bonus for a Scorpio bathroom would be a steam room. The dark, hot and watery environment appeals to a Scorpio and the steam allows them to sweat out impurities, a very plutonian pleasure.

Chapter 9: The Sagittarius Home

SAGITTARIUS

Sagittarius Description
Element: Fire
Sign Quality: Mutable
Ruling Planet: Jupiter
Zodiac House: Ninth House of Travel & Higher Education
Corporeal Representation: Liver, Hips, Pelvis & Thighs

Sagittarius represents the ninth house of the Zodiac and these people are characterized as intelligent, festive, adventurous and sometimes over indulgent. Ruled by the expansive and lucky planet Jupiter, Sagittarians tend to crave wide open spaces, new adventures and learning new things. Typically, the native Sagittarius is optimistic and generally sees the glass as half full.

The native Sagittarius has a deep connection with the great outdoors. In fact, the true Sagittarius can sometimes find it difficult to be indoors for too long! Far-away lands and knowledge are favorites of the Sagittarius native. You can almost always find a Sagittarius in a large well stocked library or off somewhere on an adventure in an exotic land.

The character Indian Jones is a perfect representation of a Sagittarius as he's an Archeologist that is a university professor, yet goes on wild adventures and always escapes crazy situations. Almost every Sagittarius will have a grand story or two to tell of some wild adventure.

The Fire Element and the Sagittarius Home

The Sagittarius loves action in the home. They will typically have roommates or guests over quite often so the space must be ripe for entertaining. When it comes to the home, Sagittarians love to bring the outdoors inside. I would call their style "Modern Rustic" because you'll see many outdoorsy items mixed with some of the latest in furniture design.

The main focal point of any Sagittarius home will have a fire element to it. Features like a fireplace or an outdoor fire pit are almost essentials for the Sagittarius home. Bright bold colors mixed with hues of nature are welcomed as well. Make sure any accent walls feature an interesting pop of color or a wild print.

Sagittarius Colors
Royal Blue
Purple
Emerald Green
Pewter
White

Sagittarius Design Materials
Cedar
Alderwood
Tin
Animal Prints
Reclaimed Woods

The Sagittarius Living Room

Entertainment is the main purpose of the Sagittarius living room, so there should be plenty of places to sit and various nooks for conversation. That way, guests can engage in lively separate conversations throughout the living space. In the central living area, the sofa should be large and comfortable and there should be at least two extra chairs for any guests that may visit.

Royal blue accent pillows add a welcome pop of color in this bright living space. Pairing the clean lines of the modern sofa and love seat with the rustic jute area rug is a great way to satisfy the Sagittarian need to mix rustic and updated pieces.

Royal blue or purple work well as accent colors in the living space. The background colors should be shades of grey and/or white to highlight the bright accents. Old wood pieces are also favored by the Sagittarius and will help bring an outdoorsy feel to the space. Sagittarians tend to love mixing the old with the new, so this juxtaposition should be featured in the living space as much as possible.

Other elements for a Sagittarius living space would be animal artifacts like those that would be found in a hunting lodge. For Sagittarians that do not like hunting or harming animals, there are lots of great faux art of animals that can be used instead. A pet would make both an excellent companion and a great accessory for the native Sagittarius as well. The more exotic the better! A rare breed of dog, a colorful reptile or even a cute pet pig would be true to the adventurous and generous nature of the Sagittarius.

Be sure to include plants as well in the living space as they provide oxygen and help marry the outdoors with the indoors. Plenty of daylight and access to an outside living space is also favored by the Sagittarius native. Large windows that let in plenty of sunlight and air are also important.

The Sagittarius Kitchen and Dining Area

The Sagittarius is not as obsessed with food as many other signs, so the kitchen does not need to be as decked out. Like the Aries, many Sagittarians would rather explore new restaurants and pubs than cook a meal at home. They do, however, love when a guest cooks as they are observant and like to taste the favorite foods of friends and family. Therefore, the kitchen must have at least the basic essentials.

Natural wood tones juxtaposed against modern design characterize this open concept kitchen/dining space. The kitchen area is moderate in size, which is perfect for the busy and active Sagittarius.

The space doesn't need to be extremely neat, but everything should to have its place, whether it is in a cupboard, or in a designated corner on the counter. Tin is the metal of the Sagittarius, so a stylish tin ceiling would make a great feature in the kitchen and give it an old-world element that the native Sagittarius would appreciate.

The dining room doesn't need to be as large either. Guests will likely eat quickly and continue the conversation or festivities back in the living space. As such, the dining room can serve as a display of their eclectic taste in rustic and modern décor. An old reclaimed wood table and some interesting, yet comfortable dining chairs would suffice. It would also make the dining area a great extra space where party guests can gather.

The Sagittarius Bedroom

The native Sagittarius rarely sleeps in. This is one of those signs that will find it easy to get up in the morning and go for a hike or hit the gym. Hence, the bedroom can be simple with just the necessities. A bed that is of adequate size, a couple of night stands and one dresser to store clothing would be just enough.

This bedroom features a modern bed against a reclaimed wood wall. The grey tones in the old wood go well with the grey bed and bedding. Note that the space has plenty of sunlight as well.

The base pallet of colors for the room would be lavender for females and a gentle grey for males. Accents can be bright pops of red, purple or royal blue. Here, rustic décor elements can be used as well. A reclaimed wood headboard would make a great design element and offer contrast to the bright pops of color.

The closet space needs to be large enough to hold the interesting pieces of clothing a Sagittarius might collect in their travels. In fact, exotic hats, shoes and other artifacts from travels can be used as décor in the bedroom or in a large walk-in closet. One thing that needs special attention in a Sagittarius closet is the recreational clothing. These items may be used more often than regular clothing, so they should be easy to access and have a separate area in the closet. Scuba gear, equestrian clothing and accessories and/or hiking gear would all likely be found in the closet of a native Sagittarius.

The Sagittarius Bathroom

Due to their active and busy lifestyle, the true Sagittarius regards the bathroom as a place of recuperation. Long hot baths and long hot showers can do wonders for their aching muscles and bones after a day of adventure, so these areas should be emphasized and represent the Sagittarius' unique style. A lovely free-standing tub and

This bathroom model features a skylight, a classic claw-foot free standing tub and warm wood floor and cabinets.

separate shower would appeal to the Sagittarius appreciation of classic style while having great utility. A free-standing sink and cabinet combination would be ideal and offer storage for bathroom supplies.

The Sagittarius is revitalized by the sun, so there should be plenty of sunlight in the bathroom. The Sagittarius is more comfortable feeling like they are outdoors even when bathing; therefore, they would greatly appreciate visibility and access to a private outdoor area off of the bathroom.

Chapter 10: The Capricorn Home

CAPRICORNUS

Capricorn Description
Element: Earth
Sign Quality: Cardinal
Ruling Planet: Saturn
Zodiac House: Tenth House of Career & Status
Corporeal Representation: Skeletal Structure, Knees & Teeth

Capricorns represent the tenth sign of the Zodiac and are generally known as solid, reliable, dependable and respectable. Anyone with a Capricorn friend knows that they have found someone they can count on. Ruled by Saturn, the planet of responsibility, structure and permanence, Capricorns represent the solid structure that stands the test of time.

Saturn rules time so you'll find that many Capricorns become more beautiful and successful later in life than most other signs. It is quite common to think a Capricorn is much younger than they look. However, the moment you hold a conversation with them, their age is very much revealed.

Represented by the Sea Goat, Capricorns work hard to slowly reach the pentacle of their careers and personal lives. If you've ever seen a goat slowly climbing a steep hill, you'll understand the nature of a Capricorn. They will climb the mountain, no matter how steep, and reach the top. In a relationship, Capricorns are loyal and totally faithful since Saturn has a strong effect on their sense of responsibility. In spite of their involvement in their career, most Capricorns eventually find the time to raise a family quite successfully.

The Earth Element and the Capricorn Home

Capricorn is certainly an earth sign and this is highly reflected in their style at home. Traditional and highly structured elements are characteristic of the Capricorn abode. A Capricorn may seem a bit cold and calculating, but they love a sense warmth and comfort in their private space. Warm colors mixed with cool colors are perfect for Capricorn and provide a sense of balance.

Floors should be hardwood or a smooth stone as this makes the native Capricorn feel more anchored. Exposed brick is another design element that the native Capricorn truly appreciates. Plenty of plants would be favored as well as decorative ceramics. Ceramics require the mix of earth and water, which appeals to the "Sea Goat" of the Zodiac.

Capricorn Colors
Brown
Green
Indigo
Dark Grey
Black

Capricorn Design Materials
Cherry Wood
Elm Wood
Brass
Leather
Dark Stone

The Capricorn Living Room

Elegant, sophisticated and traditional is the most favored styling for the Capricorn living space. Like the Leo, a Capricorn would love to have a formal living room to receive visiting friends and co-workers. This space would also make it easier to separate the less formal family area from a space that would be appropriate for colleagues and associates.

Earthy colors and materials are combined with updated classic furniture in this cozy living space. The fireplace, with its traditional mantel, is very much in line with Capricorn style.

The formal living space should provide comfortable and stylish seating with warm and inviting tones. A monochromatic scheme using neutral colors with a pop of indigo or green would work very well. The space should have magazines, interesting sculptures and art pieces that reflect the Capricorn's refined taste and appreciation for classic works of art.

The family room would be less formal, but equally stylish. The sofa can be moderately sized as a Capricorn may not have as active a family life as other signs. The family room is likely to be well organized having a place for everything. A fireplace is a much-appreciated element in the family area as Capricorns love a cozy fire where they can spend time alongside their loved ones.

A television would be appreciated in this area as well, but the native Capricorn would need all of the media and added electronics to be hidden so as not to affect the overall look of traditional coziness. Benches with storage also work very well in the Capricorn family room, mainly because it will enable them to neatly store any extras like throws and pillows.

The Capricorn Kitchen and Dining Area

A Capricorn is a traditionalist in many respects, but they are not overly concerned with cooking or food. They appreciate an efficient kitchen area that is conducive to making meals occasionally for the family or to entertain visiting associates. If they are

A small but adequate kitchen/dining room combination is perfect for Capricorns. Updated appliances, beautiful cabinetry and counter-tops all suit the Capricorn's need for order and beauty.

not adept at cooking themselves, they will certainly leave this up to the mate or a trusted cook. Hence, the kitchen area should have all of the utensils necessary for cooking.

A lovely stone floor and an earthy stone back splash are fantastic elements for a Capricorn kitchen. However, the counter-tops will need to be kept neat and clear of clutter for the space to feel comfortable to them. Fruits and/or vegetables on display are the best decorative elements you can have for the Capricorn kitchen because the busy Capricorn can grab one on the go.

The dining space is usually incorporated with the kitchen space to make cooking and eating a quick meal easy. An eat-in kitchen is ideal for the single Capricorn. However, for those Capricorns that have a family or entertain often, a formal dining space would be appreciated and well used.

The dining table should be made of wood and have comfortable upholstered chairs. A simple display case showcasing fine dinnerware would work well in the Capricorn dining room as well. If the space is a formal dining room, a large light fixture would create a great focal point and lighting for the area.

The Capricorn Bedroom

A large master suite with a separate area for work would be ideal for the Capricorn native. Note the earthy colors and rich wood tones in the space.

The bedroom is where the native Capricorn can both sleep and get work done, so you'll likely find a separate small office nook in the bedroom if they do not have a separate office space. The bed is likely to be wooden and have traditional styling. Clean white sheets and a cozy duvet-covered comforter would provide comfort and can add some color to the room if chosen correctly. Indigo, dark green or dark grey are great accent colors for a Capricorn room. Wallpaper is also appreciated by the native Capricorn. A simple print that provides an accent would suffice. Avoid brightly colored floral prints as this can be too busy a pattern for the resting place of a Capricorn.

The ideal room would have a fireplace where the Capricorn can snuggle-up in front of it and read a book before bed. Capricorns love daylight as it makes them more productive, so the room should get plenty of sunlight or be well lit. A terrace off of the bedroom where the native Capricorn can sit in the sun for a bit would be ideal.

The closet would likely be full of work clothing and shoes, many of which might still be wrapped in the protective covering from being dry cleaned. Work and special occasion clothing should have prime placement in the closet area and be easy to access. Capricorns do love recreation, but are often so busy with work they have to squeeze it in. A small area in the back of the closet where clothing needed for a quick work-out, a refreshing hike or a session of yoga is all they would need.

The Capricorn Bathroom

The bathroom is a very utilitarian space to the true Capricorn. They usually don't have the time to spend hours in the bath, but they still want the option. Therefore, a nice adequately sized tub and shower combination works well in the space. The Capricorn also appreciates plenty of storage in the bathroom where toiletries can be neatly hidden.

It is very important to the Capricorn to have ample clean towels. In fact, they love to see clean, white and fluffy towels readily available to take a quick shower or bath. Clean white subway tiles or earthy neutral colored tiles suit the Capricorn well. Fixtures can be brass or gold colored to add a sense of traditional opulence and interest.

Note the mirror over the sink in a warm gold tone. The tub and neutral palette make this bathroom look like a retreat.

Chapter 11: The Aquarius Home

AQUARIUS

Aquarius Description
Element: Air
Sign Quality: Fixed
Ruling Planet: Uranus
Zodiac House: Eleventh House of Community & Friends
Corporeal Representation: Circulatory System, Calves, Ankles, Achilies Heel & Shins

Known as "The Water Bearer" Aquarius is the ruler of the eleventh house of the zodiac. The native Aquarius is typically described as progressive, eccentric, forward-looking, quirky and unique. Although the eleventh sign represents the Zodiac's house of collective consciousness, humanitarianism, groups and organizations; the typical Aquarius tends to be very individualistic.

Most Aquarians tend to have very futuristic views on how we all should function as a collective. At times, an Aquarius can be a bit overwhelming, especially for people that are very traditional. Yet, they always seem to get even the stalest traditionalist thinking. To the true Aquarius, science and technology is the key to our future. Think of the "Age of Aquarius", which is said to represent a more consciously evolved time in human history.

The native Aquarius is ruled by the planet Uranus, which rules, freedom, sudden change, rebellion, technology and the internet. Consequently, Aquarians generally care very much about issues like human rights and the right to information. You'll also find that most Aquarians are quite knowledgeable about most electronic technology and are also likely to speak more than one language due to an innate sense of worldliness.

The Air Element and the Aquarius Home

The air element makes the typical Aquarius quite intelligent and observant. Since the Aquarian is ruled by Uranus, they are very good and shaking things up in the home and usually prefer items that are off-beat or revolutionary in some way. Technology is one of the ways that Aquarians like to express their forward-looking tendencies. You may find the latest computer technology or trendy gadget in the home as well as advanced home automation systems.

Like fellow air signs Gemini and Libra, the Aquarius thrives in spaces that get a lot of fresh air. As such, the home of the Aquarius should have many windows that can be opened. Spaciousness is more important to the Aquarius than the other air signs, so it's best to choose a home that has quite a bit of square footage. The native Aquarius also appreciates an outdoor living space and one should be incorporated where possible.

When it comes to style, the Aquarius would likely favor contemporary elements. Furniture pieces that use man-made materials such as vinyl or plastic may be preferred If you want design inspiration for an Aquarius home, you might want to take cues from the styling of the latest version of the starship enterprise from Star Trek.

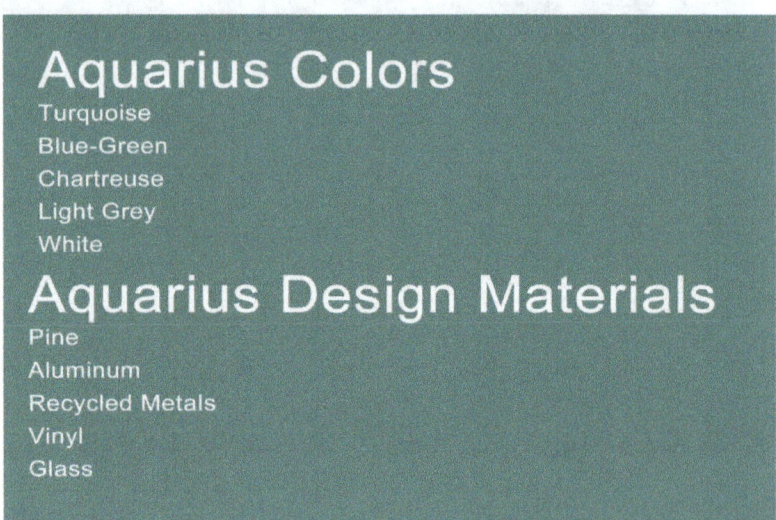

Aquarius Colors
Turquoise
Blue-Green
Chartreuse
Light Grey
White

Aquarius Design Materials
Pine
Aluminum
Recycled Metals
Vinyl
Glass

The Aquarius Living Room

The eleventh house also rules friends, so friends are very important to the Aquarius native. Therefore, the Aquarius would likely do a lot of entertaining. Due to their forward-looking nature, the entertainment for any gathering might be more focused on watching a movie or having a collaborative potluck as opposed to wild parties. Expect the entertainment area to have the latest gaming console, HD TV and/or a sound system to tie it all together.

In the photo to the left, the large windows let in plenty of light, which the Aquarius really needs. Blue accents provide a welcome and soothing element to the space. The furniture is very contemporary, reflecting the Aquarian futuristic taste.

Since the entertainment area is likely the main focus of the living space, all furniture should be oriented in a way that provides a clear view of the area.

The furniture should be very contemporary using lots of white with pops of turquoise or bright lime green. A solid colored, yet comfortable, area rug can serve to define the living/entertainment space and add a splash of color. An interesting and off-beat chair can add some flair to the living space and serve as extra seating. Consider a fun accent chair or two from the Aquarian furniture designer Arne Jacobsen. The swan chair and the egg chair are popular choices and are just as quirky as the native Aquarius.

The Aquarius kitchen and Dining Area

The Aquarius loves an open floor plan and would appreciate an expansive living space that opens to the kitchen and dining area. The kitchen space doesn't need to be

White and light-colored details are characteristic of the Aquarius preference. The mid-century modern Eames chairs at the dining table add a great feature to this space. Large widows provide the needed light and air that an Aquarius needs to thrive.

large as the Aquarius would likely eat out quite a bit. If there is an occasion to cook, it'll likely be as a party theme, so the kitchen should have everything needed for basic cooking.

Hi-tech appliances appeal to the space-aged Aquarius, as well as metal tiles and polished metal details. Smooth white quartz counter-tops and a glass tile backsplash in green-blue would make a great compliment in the kitchen space. Incorporating some type of cutting edge technology, such as a hand's free faucet in the kitchen would also be appropriate.

The dining area can be a bar height small round glass table with four contemporary stools that match the kitchen space color scheme and décor. The bar height will make the dining space look more informal and fit the open concept kitchen/dining space. A small buffet with clean lines would be useful to hold dishes and flatware. Lighting in this space should be bright, or receive plenty of daylight to attract the Aquarius to this area, as it may never be used if not properly lit.

The Aquarius Bedroom

Expansive windows and a space-aged bed are the main features in this bedroom. A true Aquarius would sleep very well in a bedroom that isn't typical or reminiscent of the norm.

Like the Virgo, the Aquarius bedroom is likely to have a minimalist look. The bed may be the only focal point in the space, so it should be of adequate size and have an interesting design. A large platform bed with interesting detail and clean simple décor works well. If the bed has storage, that would be ideal.

A large open room would be preferred with plenty of natural light. Glass adds the water element, which the Aquarius likes to incorporate in their design style, so storage with mirrored doors can serve double duty as a place to stash things and provide the water element. Mirrors also help small spaces to feel large, which would please the native Aquarius.

The ideal closet space would be all white and well lit. Sleek white shelves, cubbies and cabinets would create a clean look. The space should be expansive enough to provide plenty of room for storage. A window that provides natural light and a chance to let in fresh air would be ideal as well.

The Aquarius Bathroom

An Aquarius would greatly appreciate the holistic healing qualities of a spa, so the bathroom should look as much like a spa as possible. The general clean and sleek style of most modern spas would be the ideal inspiration when planning the bathroom

Clean lines and pristine white is the main focus of this very airy and open bathroom rendering. The bathtub is a design element in itself and the floating vanity is the epitome of simplicity and utility.

Open shelving where ample towels can be stored would be preferred and can offer a great decorative element as well.

A modern freestanding white tub with shiny metal fixtures is ideal. A separate shower area enclosed in clear glass would also appeal to the Aquarius. Another great feature in the Aquarius bathroom is a skylight that can open up to the sky. As an air sign, Aquarians need fresh air and sunlight, so this would be a very welcome extra feature.

Chapter 12: The Pisces Home

PISCES

Pisces Description
Element: Water
Sign Quality: Mutable
Ruling Planet: Neptune
Zodiac House: Twelfth House of Spirituality & Subconscience
Corporeal Representation: The Feet & Immune System

Pisces is the twelfth and last sign of the Zodiac and those of this Sun sign are characterized as selfless, ethereal, spiritual, intuitive and psychic. Ruled by Neptune the planet that represents oceans, seas, rivers and lakes, Pisceans are very fluid creatures and can adapt very easily to changing circumstances. They tend to be very sensitive to vague feelings and trends that run through the collective conscious and can have amazing, almost psychic, responses to everyday situations.

Jupiter is considered the co-ruler of Pisces as well. Jupiter is the planet of spirituality, religion, education, growth and expansion. As such, many Piscean are religious or very spiritual. The Jupiter influence on a Pisces can cause them to be altruistic, giving and forgiving on a level that few can manage. The capacity for universal love and tolerance that a true Pisces can possess can be a real marvel.

The native Pisces is a dreamy sign prone to great creative imagination, but may have a hard time putting this gift to great use. The twelfth house is the last house of the Zodiac and it represents completion and convergence of all of the signs. As a result, a Pisces can possess any of the characteristics of the previous eleven zodiac signs at any time due to their highly mutable nature. Therefore, if you are reading this chapter as a Pisces sun sign, you would do well to look at all of the chapters as your taste can vary widely and is not as easy to predict.

The Water Element and the Pisces Home

When it comes to the home, the native Pisces is not the tidiest of the signs. Due to their dreamy and watery nature, they typically are not very preoccupied with the humdrum of earthly and practical things like house cleaning, so the average Pisces home may be rather untidy. Paradoxically, some Pisceans are so aware of their tendency to drift off into the ether that they create a highly organized home where everything has its place. This makes it easy to keep it neat without having to think about it so much.

When it comes to style, the Pisces wants a home that is very cozy; a space that shields this sensitive sign from the outside world. Soft natural fabrics and hues of blue should be prevalent in the home décor. Water themes are favored and help the Pisces to relax and recuperate. For Pisces design inspiration, think of nautical, beach house, and/or shabby chic cottage themes.

Pisces Colors
Light Blue
Sea-Green
Lavender
Silver
White

Pisces Design Materials
Teak
Chrome
Raw Linen
Chiffon
Glass

The Pisces Living Room

The purpose of the living room for a Pisces is to provide a space to dream and be with family. The Pisces native will not usually have many guests as the home is a very private place for them and most are keen to keep any negative energy out of the space. They crave relaxed comfort in design and nothing too showy or pretentious.

A linen slip-covered sofa and two classic club chairs would be ideal in the space. Any upholstery can be a whimsical chintz print or a neutral color. Pillows can be a contrasting color like orange, but nothing too bold like red as extremely bold colors tend to be disturbing in a Pisces home. There should be a plain area rug and plenty of books around for them to choose from.

As for entertainment, there are two extremes with Pisces natives. One may want all of the TV equipment necessary to get lost in a great movie or one may not like a TV at all and prefer loads of books and a cozy fireplace to a noisy entertainment area. If there is an entertainment space, its needs

Casual comfort is a priority for the native Pisces. Frills and opulence provide more stress than comfort. Blue is the best color, but orange provides a great infusion of energy.

to be covered so that all electronics are only seen when they are in use.

A water element would also be welcomed in a Pisces living room. A fish tank for exotic fish or an indoor fountain would provide a comforting extra for the living space. A Pisces would find wallpaper with a beautiful and simple print enjoyable as well. Subtle floral prints, beach themed and/or lightly textured wallpaper would likely be preferred.

The Pisces Kitchen and Dining Space

These people usually don't need a large kitchen area. Ease of access to anything that is needed to make a meal is the only priority. The kitchen does, however, need to be bright and use soothing and friendly colors. Aquamarine, sea Green and wood elements would do perfectly. Cabinets need not be too large as the Pisces would not need to use many fancy kitchen devices as many of the other signs. A hardwood floor would be preferred over any stone flooring as the wood gives the feeling of warmth.

The open concept is very much preferred by the native Pisces. In this space, it is easy to transition from cooking the meal to eating it with family or friends. Observe the light colors and watery blue accents.

The dining space can be open to the kitchen so that once a meal is complete; the Pisces native and family can simply move over to the table and eat. Since Pisceans are sympathetic listeners, there are likely to be many conversations with friends over a cup of coffee or tea in this space. Therefore, the chairs should be comfortable and perhaps have decorative cushions. A simple low-profile buffet where any plates, cups and flatware can be stored would suffice.

The Pisces Bedroom

Peace and quiet is very important to the Pisces in the bedroom. The bedroom should be located in the back of the home farthest from the busier areas. Plenty of light is needed and so is darkness. The ideal window treatment would be chiffon inner curtains with heavy black-out drapery. That way, during the day the light can flood the room without too much exposure and the heavier drapes can be closed to provide

Note the softness of the bed and the light ethereal styling of the room in general. This is a more female Pisces room, but you can still model a Pisces male room after this Image by changing out the some of the colors and fabric textures.

darkness for daytime naps, which most Pisceans enjoy.

The bed can be wooden with a great relaxed beach theme. Bedding should be very light colored and provide an almost cloud-like softness. Lavender is a color that's known to be very soothing, so female Pisceans should consider this color for the bedroom décor. Males might consider a light shade of grey or taupe.

The closet space most definitely needs to be professionally organized as most Pisceans will likely not bother to organize it themselves. The closet of a Pisces can be quite a nightmare for them if there isn't some kind of organizational system incorporated. For those highly organized Pisceans who can organize the closet themselves, make sure there are plenty of storage baskets where you can separate items like scarves, socks and other items. Ample hooks where hats and robes can be hung will help as well, so that things don't end up on the floor.

The Pisces Bathroom

Like the other water signs, the Pisces native loves to take a bath. However, the need for a soothing bath is much more frequent than any of the other water signs. The bathtub should be the most expensive investment in the space. A free-standing cast iron tub would be the best option, but a modern stone tub would work as well.

The tub is the main focal point in this bright and serene bathroom. The tub is also deep enabling the Pisces native to be totally immersed if they choose.

Great design inspiration for a Pisces bathroom would be a meadow with a pond in the spring. The colors should be white, silver, light blue or blue-green in this space and it should be as warm as possible. Radiant heat floors would provide an appreciated extra. Wood or warm-toned cabinets would work as storage and provide contrast to the lighter, more watery colors.

Chapter 13: What You've Learned and How to Use It

By now, you should have read the chapters on the design and style recommendations for your sun sign, rising sign and the sign(s) prevalent in your fourth house. As you read through them, there may have been recommended design elements that you absolutely loved and some that you didn't. Put aside the recommendations that you didn't favor and focus on the recommendations that you found most compelling.

On the next page, there is a simple worksheet that is designed to help you note the style elements that you loved the most in one easy document. For those that have the eBook version, you can use the worksheet as a model to create your own version. If you purchased the print version, you can fill in the worksheet in the book or make copies to use the worksheet many times. Once the worksheet is filled in, you'll have a comprehensive guide that includes colors, textures, decorative styles and design materials you prefer for your home.

In the "Zodiac Reference" column, you'll see rows below for the sun sign, ascendant sign and the fourth house sign(s). Fill out each of the columns in each row with what you discovered/liked. Starting with your sun sign, fill in the requested information and continue the same process for your ascendant and fourth house signs.

Colors: These would be the recommended colors that you liked.

Design Materials: This would be the hard materials that were recommended e.g. woods, metals, fabrics, wallpaper, ceramics etc.

Overall Style: This would be one of the fundamental design styles that were recommended, e.g. mid-century modern, contemporary, traditional, shabby chic or any other general descriptions (opulent, simple, clean, embellished etc.)

Your Personal Design and Décor Guide

Use this table for noting the décor and design elements you liked.

Zodiac Reference	Colors	Design Materials	Overall Style
Sun Sign			
Ascendant Sign			
Fourth House Sign(s)			

Extra Notes:
_____

References

General definition of Astrology, 2014, cited from: http://en.wikipedia.org/wiki/Astrology

General information on the Zodiac, 2014, cited from: http://en.wikipedia.org/wiki/Zodiac

Description of the 12 Signs, 2014, retrieved from: http://en.wikipedia.org/wiki/Zodiac#The_twelve_signs

Description of the Fire element, 2014, from: http://www.astrology.com/fire-0/2-d-d-67460

Description of the Water element, 2014, from: http://www.astrology.com/water/2-d-d-67461

Description of the Air element, 2014, from: http://www.astrology.com/air/2-d-d-67446

Description of the Earth element, 2014, from: http://www.astrology.com/earth/2-d-d-67459

General definition of the Ascendant, 2014, from: http://www.merriam-webster.com/dictionary/ascendent

Information on origin of fabrics for general Zodiac reference, 2014, from: http://www.textileschool.com/articles/339/history-of-fabrics

The Zodiac sign representation of various countries, 2014, from: http://www.astrologyweekly.com/more-horary/countries-cities.php

Zodiac sign wood types, 2014, from: http://www.wizardwands.net/zodiac-guide.htm

Zodiac sign colors, 2014, from: xstrologyscopes.com (Click on the pages on each sign to locate the link to each sign's colors)

Reference for the general description of each Zodiac sign, 2014, from: http://www.horoscopeswithin.com/sunsigns.php

Reference for the general information on the Sun signs, 2014, from: http://www.astrology.com

Photo Credits

Cover Photo provided by iStock.com contributors: Katarzyna Bialasiewicz.
Cover art created by Shekita Williams.

About the Author: Portrait of Kita Marie Williams by Joshua Freedman of Freedman Photography.

Introduction: Stock photos from BigStock.com contributors: CandyBox Images, Gudella, Peter Hermes Furian.

Zodiac symbols for all of the chapters provided by BigStock.com contributor Peter Hermes Furian.

The Aries Home photos by: Page 14 Photo by Joshua Freedman of Freedman Photography other photos from BigStock.com contributors: Baloncici, Hannamariah and LuckyPhoto.

The Taurus Home photos from BigStock.com contributors: pics721, Rodenberg, nruboc and Nosnibor137.

The Gemini Home photos from BigStock.com contributors: Sklep Spozywczy, karamysh, Nosnibor137, ffennema and AntClausen.

The Cancer Home photos from BigStock.com contributors: Rodenberg. Morguefile photo contributor: Gracey.

The Leo Home photos from BigStock.com contributors: Santiago Cornejo, WPCasey, Victoria Andreas and Nruboc.

The Virgo Home photos from BigStock.com contributors: Slidezero, Santiago Cornejo, PlusONE and Rodenberg

The Libra Home photos from BigStock.com contributors: Yampi, Kasia Bialasiewicz and PlusONE.

The Scorpio Home photos from BigStock.com contributors: Nruboc, Melis, Baloncici and Artkorad.

The Sagittarius Home photos from BigStock.com contributors: PlusONE, Rodenberg and Kasia Bialasiewicz.

The Capricorn Home photos from BigStock.com contributors: Rodenberg and Tomaszm.

The Aquarius Home photos from BigStock.com contributors: PlusONE

The Pisces Home photos from BigStock.com contributors: Rodenberg, Hannamariah, Karamysh and viczast.

www.ingramcontent.com/pod-product-compliance
Lightning Source LLC
Chambersburg PA
CBHW081156290426
44108CB00018B/2572